SPIRITUAL GIFTS FOR CHRISTIANS TODAY

SPIRITUAL GIFTS
FOR CHRISTIANS TODAY

Knofel Staton

College Press Publishing Company, Joplin, Missouri

Copyright © 1973
College Press
Revision and Reprint 1974
Reprint 1979
Reprint 1986

Cover design by Dan DeWelt

ISBN: 0-89900-134-3

This book is dedicated
to Elsie DeWelt,
whose partnership has helped
Don DeWelt to dedicate
his life and works
to Christ.

LESSONS

1) A Look at Supernatural Experiences .... page 13

2) Christian Reaction Toward Potential and Practicing Tongue-Speakers .... page 33

3) An In-Depth Look at the "Perfect" of I Corinthians 13 .... page 47

4) An In-Depth Look at "Know Fully" In I Corinthians 13:12 .... page 57

5) An In-Depth Look at "Tongues" in the Bible .... page 65

6) A Look at I Corinthians 14 in Its Literary Context .... page 73

7) A Look at Some of the Texts and Logic of the Glossolalists .... page 95

8) The Christian's Charisma .... page 115

INTRODUCTION

Much is being written about the current glossolalia movement, with special emphasis upon speaking in tongues. With so much coming off the presses one might wonder why the need for another treatise on the subject. It is my intention in this discussion to deal with some of the issues not often covered in-depth among current writers. Despite all which is being written, both pro and con, many people use the experiences they have or have not had to evaluate the current situation. Lessons 1 and 2 deal with this problem. Lesson 1 gives evidence for the need of using caution in basing belief upon experiences only. Lesson 2 cautions the non-glossolalists against judging the glossolalists on the basis of experiences the former have not encountered. Perhaps no topic is more needed in the study of spiritual gifts than the topic of Lesson 2. Lessons 3-5 look objectively at some exegetical points which need to be considered.

These lessons were written to complement other works, not to condemn them or to consider them to be unworthy. I began this work knowing my presuppositions. We all have them. They can easily become a "box" in which we live. It is too easy to bend exegesis to fit our pre-drawn conclusion. I determined to be as objective as I could humanly be, knowing the limitations in doing even that. However, I decided to let the exegesis lead me to a conclusion rather than vice versa. I only hope the reader of these lessons will do the same. I ask that the critic attack the work on the basis of an objective Greek exegesis.

Lesson 6 discusses 1 Corinthians 14 in its literary context. Understanding the text without studying the context is perhaps the most common error of all. I hope this lesson will be a contribution to the understanding of some of Paul's first letter to the church at Corinth. Lesson 7 considers some of the logic of glossolalists and is the least complete study of this treatise. Lesson 8 is perhaps the very most important since each Christian wants *charisma*. An understanding of how *charisma* is used in the New Testament and how each Christian relates to *charisma* is a needed emphasis for today.

This work was written to encourage the reader to study the texts discussed. If it succeeds in causing the reader to read and re-read these texts, all of them referred to, it will have been worth the time in writing. If it causes us to better accept the *self* God made in us and to live in more harmony with those who differ from us, it will be worth all the criticism I shall receive for having written it.

The subject of the Holy Spirit must not be restricted to

INTRODUCTION

one aspect of his work, as this book and most such books do. The reader may want to consider also my book, *Don't Divorce the Holy Spirit* (Standard) for an overview of the Spirit's activity in the entire Bible.

I am particularly indebted to Don DeWelt, who read these lessons in mimeographed form when they first appeared in the *Chapel News* of Ozark Bible College. Mr. DeWelt decided to give the essays a broader audience than the students for whom they were first written. For that confidence from a man who has spent more than 30 years studying the Holy Spirit and has written 4 books on the subject, I am humbled.

Knofel Staton

1

A LOOK AT "SUPERNATURAL" EXPERIENCES

Various phenomena which appear to have a suprahuman source are daily being reported within Christianity. Speaking in tongues *(glossolalia),* predictions about the future *(prophecies),* supernatural voices and visions *(theophanies),* casting out demons *(exorcism),* pronouncing curses *(defixiones),* healings, etc. are being considered by some to be objectively validating the power of the God of Christianity.

We cannot deny the existence of these experiences. *Something* is happening. However, the question is "What?" We wonder—Is this a restoration of New Testament Christianity? On the surface, *it appears to be!* But before making an *a priori* decision, we must take a closer look at the interpretation of "supernatural" experiences.

Several questions need consideration—

(1) Were these kinds of phenomena ever a part of Christianity? *The answer is obviously yes.*

(2) Are these kinds of phenomena to be a continuous part of Christianity? *The answer is debatable.*

(3) Are these phenomena experienced outside Christianity? *The answer is definitely yes,* as will be demonstrated in this study.

With the affirmation of this last question, Christians should be cautious about interpreting the source of *their* experiences. The reason is obvious—if "supernatural" experiences *per se* validate the gods of the pagan religions which also manifest them!

That leaves us with this dilemma—how do we interpret "supernatural" phenomena? If the experience itself validates deity, then one man's deity validated by the supernatural phenomenon he has personally experienced is as good as another man's god validated by the same criterion. We are then left with a multiplicity of *true* religions with "gods" validated by "miraculous powers." Therefore, the Christian's Bible cannot stand as unique; monotheism will have to go; and the Jesus of history lied when He claimed that only through Him can humans know the one God and come to Him. Christians who do not want to admit these conclusions, which logically follow from the premise of validation of religion by miracles *only,* must not be overly zealous to attribute all of *their* special experiences to God!

It is my intention in this lesson to do three things:

(1) To show that the "supernatural" experiences being reported within Christianity today have their parallels within pagan religions.

(2) To suggest some explanations for this.
(3) To make some concluding evaluations.

I. PAGAN PHENOMENA

T.K. Oesterreich's book *Possession: Demoniacal and Other Among Primitive Races, in Antiquity, the Middle Ages, and Modern Times* is a classic in the study of case histories of religious phenomena from primary sources. Oesterreich compiled a definitive survey of "possessions" among a wide scope of both times and cultures. This work was first published in Germany in 1921, and apparently was not written with the current glossolalia movement in mind. I question Oesterreich's basic presupposition; he attributes all possessions to some sort of self-suggestion. Oesterreich doesn't seem to believe in the supra-natural, especially in demons. He does not call all possessions fake or delusions but does believe that they have a psychosomatic source. Although I cannot agree with either his presupposition or his conclusion, *I do believe that Christians must take seriously the kind of case studies he has recorded!*

Oesterreich records case studies which show pagans speaking in ecstatic utterances and in foreign languages, making predictions, casting out demons, pronouncing curses, etc. There is virtually no place on the earth where these kinds of phenomena have not been *and are not still being practiced* with "success." How can this be?

A wide-spread belief in the power of spirits (both good and evil spirits) is common in most cultures. People in many cultures have been thought to be "possessed." Several differing manifestations have accompanied demon possession:

(1) *A physical change* may take place in the person. This is

seen in various possibilities: (a) A countenance change, or (b) A new behaviour pattern, or (c) A voice change, seen in either a change in intonation or a change in content. Sometimes the change is from a male voice to a female voice, or vice versa. Sometimes the content changes from vulgarity to holy words, or vice versa. Sometimes the content becomes a howling crying, groaning, ecstatic utterance, or a foreign language.

(2) *A motor-movement change* may take place in the possessed person. This has been observed in such activities as shaking, twisting, contortions, jerking, dancing, an increase in physical strength, etc. [These kinds of motor-movements and physical changes are today being reported within Christianity and are being considered by some to validate the presence of the Holy Spirit.]

Let us now look at some specific experiences reported in pagan religions and cited by Oesterreich. In parentheses are listed the page numbers in the book where these experiences are reported.

HEALINGS

On the Tonga islands, healings were done by raising over the head of the sick person a basket containing a bead necklace, bangles and leaves of a Na tree (250). In Ceylon, people were healed by visiting the temple of the demon *Vakula Bandara Devijo* at Alcitmuvera (216). In India, some were healed in conjunction with pagan ceremonies at the temple of *Hur-hureshvurku* at Conkon (215). Other regained health by the sight of *Maya*. Others attributed their healing to the mother of Buddha (174).

I personally know a black man who for 20 years was a witch doctor in the former Biafra. He told me about healing people by a pronouncement. That is, "At such a time *you will become well.*" And they did.

In many places today, healings are being done by casting out demons. Exorcism is currently becoming popular among some Christians.

EXORCISM

In Siam, pagan "doctors" cast out demons by pronouncing charms and beating the person possessed by demons with rods (217ff). In China, gifted people called *mediums* cast out demons by entering into a communion with the departed dead (219). In Japan, the pagan sect *Nichiren* made exorcism a specialty, and people went to a temple at Nalayama for it (225). In Mecca, the spirit *Zor* was cast out by the *shechah,* who used charms and sacrifices. The Mohammedans cast out *Zor* by drinking beer, dancing, and banging their heads against a wall (234). Among the Hindus in India, demons were cast out on the 45th and 46th nights of Cukasaptati by saying, *"In the name of* Katagara, *come forth!"* Then the demon would come out, saying, *"See, I am coming forthwith"* (*174—Katagara* was the name of the wife of the Brahman who lived at Vatsamin at that time).

In Abyssinia, the evil spirit *Baudah* was cast out by a special minister, who would pour garlic juice into the nose of the possessed and have him bite a donkey, drink a secret mixture, and carry a stone on his head. It is interesting that this special minister would ask the demon what it took to cast it out, and then would follow the demon's instructions. In S.E.

Africa among the Bo-Ronga (a people then near Delagara), the evil spirit was cast out by waving a large palm leaf in front of the people (140). During the new moon, a witch would play a tamborine with the skin of a lizard, and the Bo-Ronga people would chant until the demons came out. Sometimes this lasted for weeks (143). In Madagascar, the evil demon *Saccare* was cast out by a special dance (138).

Exorcism was a common practice among Roman Catholics in earlier days. A statue of the Mother of God was used, as well as a crucifix (24). Bernard of Clairvaux would pray, put wine on the possessed person's lips, use the sign of the cross, and hold the crucifix over the head of the one possessed (177ff.). St. Francis of Assisi used prayer and the sign of the cross. He didn't even use the name of Jesus but would say, *"In virtue of obedience, I bid thee go out of her, thou unclean spirit."* And it did (182). Francis even appealed to Brother Juniper. The demons would flee at Brother Juniper's appearance. When Francis had difficulty casting out a demon, he would as a last resort say, *"If thou come not out of this creature of God straightway, I will send for* Brother Juniper *to deal with thee."* And then the demons would flee because (according to the report) they feared Juniper (182). It was a common practice for people to go to the priests for exorcisms.

NOTE: Christians today must be cautious about validating too much by *their* power to "cast out demons." If the Christian claims that this action verifies his power (a baptism of the Holy Spirit, or a spiritual gift) and verifies his God, then what about the special pagan mediums in Ceylon, India, China, Japan, etc.? What about the power of charms, beer-drinking, dancing, biting a donkey, carrying a stone on the head, waving a palm leaf, using the statue of "the Mother of God," the sign of the cross, the crucifix, the power of Katagara and of Brother Juniper? *If supernatural experiences per se determine reality, then the Christian who practices exorcism must accept the equal proofs of pagan religions which also practice exorcism with "success."*

TONGUES

E.R. Dodds in *The Greeks and the Irrational* has documented evidence that ecstatic utterances attributed to divine spirits were practiced among the Hittites as early as 1400 B.C. (69). In Greece, ecstatic utterances are as old as the religion of Apollo at Delphi (centuries before Christ). In that religion, it was believed that the "god" entered the vocal cords and controlled the speech (70). Other before-Christ Greek religions that practiced tongue-speaking were the Cassondra, Bakis, Cybele, Dionysius, Eurycles, and Pythos *(Acts 16:16ff is an example of a person possessed by the* Python *spirit).*

Oesterreich also cites pagans practicing tongue-speaking. Tongue-speaking was a part of some religions in East Africa. There it was believed that the tongue-speaking was caused by the spirit *Mpepo,* a kind of vampire spirit. Some people claimed to speak in a legitimate foreign language—either Swahili or English, and could not be convinced that it was not a foreign language even though they did not understand it (137). The Kabyles in Africa reportedly spoke in "strange voices" (133ff). Ecstatic utterances are still common among some pagan religions, and the experience is still attributed to the power of a deity taking control of the vocal cords.

In the first century, ecstatic utterances were common. *If the tongue-speaking in Acts 2 was nothing more than ecstatic utterances, the appearance would hardly have been a sign of a new age dawning,* for that kind of phenomenon had been around since before the days of the Exodus.

But what about someone who begins to speak in a legitimate foreign language which he had never learned? What would *that* validate today? Before we rush into a conclusion about this, perhaps we should look at an interesting case history recorded by LeMaitre in 1906 (70ff). This is a case history about a 14-year-old boy named Fritz, who believed he was possessed by the spirit of someone named Algar. Fritz and Algar's spirit told Fritz to speak in Latin which Fritz did not know nor had studied. Nevertheless, it was verified by witnesses that Fritz spoke *in good Latin!* How could he do it?

After close study, it was discovered that when Fritz was 4 or 5 years old, he had heard a servant speak the Latin poetry that he had spoken for Algar's spirit. His subconscious had never forgotten it, although he had not remembered that he had been exposed to it.

We are now understanding that our mind stores everything it receives—even information which we are not aware we are receiving. In my judgment, we can expect to hear more Christian glossolalists speak in known languages which they have not consciously learned. But that does not mean they have not been exposed to them. Because of mass media, hardly a day goes by that we do not hear foreign languages being spoken in a newscast, movie, song, etc. Our mind will never forget that. We will need to be extremely careful about attributing an unlearned foreign language spoken under certain conditions to an external supernatural power taking control of the speech.

PREDICTIONS

What about predictions which come true? In the Fritz/Algar case, Algar's spirit predicted some of Fritz's actions before they happened, and they happened just as predicted (72). My Biafra friend told me about the times when he would tell a person, "*You will die* at such a time." And the person died. This kind of prediction is common today among animistic religions.

II. SUGGESTED EXPLANATIONS

Individual Explanations

In light of the above kinds of phenomena, many questions are raised. For example, Do good and evil spirits really exist? Is a supernatural spirit present in every case in a disease-exorcism-healing combination?

The New Testament affirms the reality of supernatural beings (angels, demons, rulers of the air, principalities, etc.); however, the conclusion that real demons are present in all the cases where exorcism works is problematic. If they are then do the pagan methods have power over demons? Perhaps Christians should remain open to other explanations about the cause and cure than those suggested by religious leaders, whether pagan or Christian.

The physical manifestation of being "possessed" could be caused by (1) an actual possession by a real demon, or by (2) a psychosomatic phenomenon. In the latter, the person is not possessed by a real demon, but psychologically is in a different state than before a special manifestation appeared in his life. In some cases, this state may be the result of some kind of auto-suggestion to fill a personal need. In some cases it would be the breaking through of a dual personality. In some cases it could be hallucinatory (i.e., the person constructs a cause and then incarnates it). In some cases, it could be fake.

It is interesting that in many cases the person who speaks audibly (or the supernatural voice which "speaks") does not give any truth he did not already know, hesitates to answer differently from what he normally would have, parallels his own sentiments, uses a voice of a person known to him and uses a language he has heard before.

After considering possible explanations for demon possession, a parallel question is, what is the explanation for successful exorcisms? There are two possible explanations: (1) demons *have* been cast out, or (2) demons *have not* been cast out. If the latter is true in any of the cases, how can we account for changes in the exorcised people? Either the real demon just wanted the person to believe that he had been cast out (*Satan is a chief deceiver*), or the change is due to auto-suggestion. If a person believes strongly enough in the power of exorcism because he has learned about that power in his culture, he may change accordingly. This is the power of mind over matter—we use that power today when we give "sugar pills" to people who believe they are sick. But wouldn't the sound of the demon's voice deny this second explanation? Not necessarily. The audible voice *could be* a "compulsive excitement of the vocal cords from the person himself" (Oesterreich, page 65). In short, some of the results may be learned responses.

A LOOK AT SUPERNATURAL EXPERIENCES

I personally observed the power of learned responses at a Pentecostal meeting I recently attended. After many people came forward for "healing," the speaker spent 15 minutes telling them about those in the past who "fell on the ground" when the Holy Spirit possessed them (He didn't tell them that this is also a common experience today among pagan people possessed by evil spirits). I kept asking myself, "Why is he spending so much time on this?" And I soon learned why. After the 15-minute review, the "healer" began to touch those who had come forward. And what do you think they did? They, of course, fell on the floor. That act helped reinforce the "healer's" reputation. But, I wonder how many of those who fell would have fallen had they not learned in advance that *this was the expected response?*

But what about predictions which come true? It is common for animistic witch doctors to pronounce sickness, health, and death. Their pronouncements often come true. Why? It seems to be the power of mind over matter. When we believe strongly in the power of the one who made a prediction concerning us, we may fulfill it. The person who believes that he will die, may die, if for no other reason than that he thought he would and was literally "scared to death."

But what about a prediction not given by a witch doctor, but heard by a spirit who talked audibly with a person? This happened between Fritz and Algar's spirit. Oesterreich called the prediction an "intention tendency" of Fritz; i.e., Fritz subconsciously intended to do something in advance, and then suggested it to himself through Algar's spirit. The fulfillment of the prediction was the realization of the tendency (72-74). If this is not close to the fact, then many witch doctors today may possess supernatural powers.

Environmental Explanations

Are there any environmental reasons for the outbreak of supernatural experiences within Christianity in this 20th century? Does the present world-view contribute anything to our understanding of these phenomena?

We have one of the best possible explanations of current developments in a parallel event in Greek history. Centuries before Christ, the Greeks were deeply engaged in experiencing supernatural phenomena. They welcomed being possessed. They called it "madness" and felt that the "madness" glorified their gods. This "madness" was expressed in such ways as dancing and ecstatic utterances. Through these kinds of manifestations, the people became assured that their gods accepted them. These manifestations served as a catharsis—a feeling of being cleansed from the guilt of sin. From this standpoint, the experiences had therapeutic value for a particular time in their history.

Because of sin, the Greeks naturally had guilt. However, not having the Bible and the Church, they had no real solution for their guilt (just as in all non-Christian religions today). However, man is forced by guilt to *do something* with it. The souls of sinful men are restless. One thing the guilty seeks and needs is assurance. Greeks sought this assurance by seeking the approval of their deities. Note that men can also gain assurance by rationalizing their sinful actions; the Greeks later did this during their Age of Enlightenment just as many of us do today. This approval from the deity would come to the Greeks in the form of "supernatural manifestations." Dodds says, *"Greek society could scarcely have endured the tensions to which it was subjected in the archaic age."* The crushing sense of human ignorance and human insecurity with the dread of divine wrath would have been unendurable without an assurance of the divine. *"Out of his divine knowledge, Apollo would tell you what to do when you felt anxious or frightened."* Dodds makes this comment, *"The Greeks believed in their Oracle, not because they were superstitious fools, but because they could not do without believing in it"* (75). He says that when this religious practice declined later, it wasn't because they didn't believe in the deity, but because other forms of religious reassurance became available (75).

What does that say about the "need" for supernatural manifestations by some Christians today? (It may even say something about the felt need of some Christians to repeatedly rededicate themselves before audiences.) The need for those kinds of experiences in order to feel right with God may be an indication that we are a bit immature in trusting the means God has given us for assurance. His Word promises us cleansing in Jesus Christ. In Him, we have eternal life (I John 5:11ff), forgiveness, and the Holy Spirit (Acts 2:38). In Him, *there is no condemnation* (Rom. 8:1). We should not have to feel insecure in our status with God (I Peter 1:3-5; II Peter 1:3-15).

In an *Ozark Bible College* chapel service, Don DeWelt suggested that the problem with many of us is that we do not really like ourselves. But if God has accepted us, *then we need to accept self* and love self. In short, we need to accept the fact that *God has cleansed us.* And then live like it (Gal. 5:25)! Paul Tillich has said it well, "the unacceptable *accepts* God's acceptance." A continual feeling of guilt, or of uncertainty, or of inferiority, can cause individuals to seek after other assurance. Because the mere written promise of God is hard to accept, they want more. Some want to hear an audible voice, or do a miraculous thing. And if they want that badly enough, it will probably come. *But from whom has it come?*

What would cause a mass interest in the glossolalia movement today when we have God's assurance in the recorded Christ-event? Again, a review of some Greek history may help us (See Dodds' chapter *Rationalism and Reaction in the Classical Age).*

Several centuries before Christ, when the Greeks were depending upon the experiential for assurance from their gods, a new kind of world-view began to appear which eventually permeated the Greek culture. *That world-view was intellectualism.* It began in the 6th century B.C. with the rise of the scientific method. This began a Greek *Age of Enlightenment* which stressed the rational. Rationalism and Naturalism became the thinking of the day. Greek scientists such as Hercataeus, Heraclitus, Anaxagoras, Democritus, and Xenophanes questioned the reality of supernatural. They made fun of catharsis. They chided the idea of demons. They suggested that it was time for man to grow up and come of age. They felt no need for the "supernatural."

This stress on the rational poured into their culture such things as naturalism, humanism, ethical permissiveness, liberation from laws, relativity instead of absolutes, and self-assertion. Some even formed dining clubs to worship Satan. The Greek *Age of Enlightenment* affected their culture in the following ways—

1. It caused a sharp polarity between the intellectual (who did not believe in the supernatural), and the common people (who did believe)—*this same thing happens today.* Intellec-

tuals were persecuted on religious grounds. Heresy trials were conducted. [Today some Christian reaction against scholarship is so sharp that some Christians believe graduate education is evil. A man who has an earned doctorate degree is often under suspicion. Accreditation for schools is questioned just because of "accreditation."]

2. It introduced wide-spread immorality based upon the freedom of the self. Many quotes from that period of time will reveal this (187):

> "Kick up our heels, laugh at the world, take no shame for anything." "Nature willed it." "Nature pays no heed to rules." "There is nothing shameful but thinking makes it so." "The body is made for immorality."

This same kind of rationalization for immoral ethics is being taught today. Dodds rightly notes that this Greek age of enlightenment "did not enable men to behave like beasts—men have always been able to do that. But it enabled them to justify their brutality" (191).

3. It introduced Satan-worship. (*And we have that today.*)

4. It left man to his own passions. (*We have done that also.*)

5. It initiated a reaction which stressed the subjective emotional experiences even more strongly than before. (This parallels the Christian glossolalia movement today.)

We need to look at this Greek religious reaction a bit more closely. The intellectuals were demanding proof and the supernaturalists were producing it. The increase in the demand for the special manifestations is seen in (1) an increased demand for magical healing, (2) the multiplication of cults which stressed a highly emotional manifestation (It was during this period that such cults as Cybele and Dionysius began, and (3) the placing of curses upon people (Dodds, page 192ff).

This magical emphasis checked the influence of the Greeks' *enlightenment* among some believers, for it gave them an assurance at a time when their ground for assurance was questioned and denied by many; i.e., this proved to them that their gods *did exist.* It permitted two ways of thinking to exist side-by-side. It eventually regressed the *Age of Enlightenment,* and another such age did not come until the 16th century! Today, it is we who are living in the wake of *that* age, and reacting to it.

In summary, what Greek rationalism poured into its culture is the same kind of effect our rationalism has poured into our culture. And the same way those Greeks who believed in the supernatural reacted against anti-supernatural intellectualism is the same way some Christians are reacting against it today, by demanding a special showing of God's power. When we begin to think that intellectualism has taken away from us the assurance of God which He has provided, we are left needing to be reassured or we quit believing. At this point, we should not forget Paul's advice, *"For the Jews demand signs and Greeks seek wisdom,* but we preach Christ crucified . . ." (I Cor. 1:22, 23).

It seems to me that the present glossolalia stress within Christianity is a direct reaction against the liberal philosophy and theology which has come out of *our* period of enlightenment (Church history confirms that glossolalia has emerged within those sporadic periods during which ritualism, formalism, and doubt arose). The current movement may be the human attempt to verify the existence of God in a time when God is being widely questioned by many. The verification is sought by a return to the miraculous past.

Thus, what Dodds said about the Greek enlightenment may be said likewise about ours, "I am inclined to conclude that one effect of the Enlightenment was to provoke in the second generation a revival of magic" (195). That revival is being seen today not only in the glossolalia movement, but also in a renewed interest in astronomy (horoscopes), fortune-tellers, witchcraft, healings, ESP, communion with the dead, palm-reading, etc. Because of the stress on naturalism, some may have sub-consciously (for self-assurance) been driven to demand "proofs of God's acceptance" of them. But rather than look for the answer in God's Word, some look for assurance in miraculous experiences.

CONCLUDING REMARKS

Christians must take a more careful look at the Bible as the Word of God and believe it! God has promised His acceptance of us in Jesus Christ. His promise is His assurance, for it has the validation of the resurrection—both Christ's and ours. In Christ, God has promised forgiveness, cleansing, the Holy Spirit, endurance, communion, and acceptance.

Casting "demons" out of Christians is a problematic activity. We do not have New Testament evidence that demons live in people *after they become Christians.* On the contrary, we are led to believe that demons cannot exist side-by-side with the Holy Spirit.

But what about demons in non-Christians? *The best way to cast demons out* of non-Christians is to preach the crucified Christ, then to fellowship and to continually educate the converted. That activity can lead men to faith in Christ, to repentance from sins, to a confession of Jesus, and to baptism into Christ, and to a life of praising God. The early church fathers believed that baptism in the divine name drove out demons. When Christ is put on (Gal. 3:26,27), the demons leave because they can have nothing to do with Him (Matt. 8:30). *"What accord has Christ with Belial?"* (II Cor. 6:15).

The one who is *in Christ* becomes a temple of God (read I Cor. 6:19). He has been transferred into a new Kingdom (Col. 1:13). In that Kingdom, he has entered into a battle against the demonic which is in the world, but not in the Christian. The weapons of the Christian in this warfare are different from exorcism (Eph. 6:10ff.). It is in fellowship with other Christians that one is further equipped for an effective warfare. Prayer, fellowship, worship, and education based upon God's Word—these are our supply depot. We are to supply one another (Heb. 10:23-25; Acts 2:42).

It is true that the Christian is to be involved in those activities which will abolish whatever stands between another man and God. This is our ministry of reconciliation (II Cor. 5:17-20). That ministry is the activity of being a peacemaker (Matt. 5:9). Peace comes to people as they are introduced to Christ, who is our peace (Rom. 5:1; Eph. 2:14; Col. 3:15; Acts 10:36). The early Christians seemed to understand that this ministry was the activity of proclaiming the crucified Christ and sharing with "crucified" Christians.

It is certainly understandable that Christians want evidence for believing in a supernatural God when the world-view teaches against such a reality. WE HAVE THAT EVIDENCE in His Word and His indwelling Spirit (II Peter 1:3-15;

Eph. 1:11-14; II Cor. 1:21; I Peter 1:3-21). If we begin to doubt it, our reassurance becomes shaky. Then we may seek added reassurance. But why? If we have been cleansed in Christ, let us accept our cleansing and get on with a life of assurance, security, and trust, seen in fellowship and service. Let us not quench God's Spirit in us (I Thess. 5:19), but rather continue being filled by His Spirit (Eph. 5:18).

One way to do that is seen in Eph. 5:19—*"by addressing one another in psalms and hymns and spiritual songs, singing and making melody to the Lord with all your heart, always and for everything giving thanks in the name of our Lord Jesus Christ to God the Father."*

DISCUSSION QUESTIONS

1. In light of the evidence of pagan experiences with exorcism, healing, tongue speaking, etc., what caution should the Christian exercise in explaining these phenomena when done by either Christians or non-Christians?

2. How early in history do we know about ecstatic tongue-speaking? What could be the explanation?

3. What are possible explanations for "demon possessions"? for exorcisms? for predictions? for speaking in a language not consciously heard by the speaker?

4. Discuss the personal need on the part of some for supernatural experiences. How do these experiences meet those needs?

5. What parallels does our culture have with the Greek period of enlightenment which gave rise to the "need" of supernatural experiences?

6. If special experiences are needed for personal assurances, what does that say about the assurances of God's promises in the Bible? of the resurrection of Jesus?

2

CHRISTIAN REACTION TOWARD POTENTIAL AND PRACTICING TONGUE-SPEAKERS

The reaction of the Christian toward tongue-speakers is as important to consider as the action of Christians with tongues. It is quite easy to react either for or against tongue-speakers without having gone through the discipline of a serious study of the issue. The Christian must not react to a tongue-speaking Christian experientially, i.e., I accept him as a brother or I don't accept him as a brother *because I have experienced tongues or because I have not.*

One of the most dangerous developments of the present charismatic movement is the trend to recognize any person as a bona-fide Christian on the basis of his experience with tongues. Some consider this phenomenon to be an essential mark of a Christian. Thus those who speak in tongues are calling themselves "The Body of Christ." A person's doctrine is of little concern. Mark 16:17 is being used as a measuring rod of the Christian, "And these signs will accompany those who believe: in my name they will cast out demons; they will speak in new tongues." Whether this passage should be so used is questionable. It is interesting that later the apostles never suggested that these signs should be used to evaluate a believer; yet they wrote at a time when false prophets were many. The book of I John is dealing with tests for identifying a Christian, but John does not mention the signs in Mark 16.

Jesus said that some of those He never knew *would cast out demons and do mighty works in His name* (Matt. 7:22,23). He said that false Christs and false prophets would come and try to lead the elect astray by mighty signs (Matt. 24:24). Paul warned the Thessalonians that the activity of Satan will be with all power and with pretended signs and wonders (II Thess. 2:9).

In none of these exhortations were the signs of Mark 16 used as a measuring rod. Why? Mark 16:9-20 was probably not a part of Mark's gospel in the 2nd century—after Mark had died. We do not say this because we do not want to accept what the Bible says, but because *we do want to accept what the Bible says.* We want to follow what the Bible says, not what a scribe added years later. The question is not will it fit our tradition but rather will it fit the text. Those who keep Mark 16:9-20 in the text do so in disregard to the manuscript evidence in order to support a tradition which is not Biblical (which is also probably the reason it was added in the first place).

Our earliest Greek manuscripts do not have Mark 16:9-20. Some early Church Fathers state that this section is not in any Greek manuscript of Mark which they have. Many of the later manuscripts which did include the section do it with the scribal mark which indicates to the reader that the section they are about to read is a spurious addition to the original document. From the standpoint of the Greek language, alone, the style of 16:9-20 suggests that it was written by a person other than the one who wrote the rest of the book of Mark.

If one will not accept the evidence of the manuscripts and the conclusions above, he should at least be consistent in his practice. If he takes Mark 16:17 to justify tongue-speaking, he should also take 16:18 which says, "they will pick up serpents, and if they drink any deadly thing, it will not hurt them; they will lay their hands on the sick, and they will recover." I suggest the latter part of this begin to be practiced in the hospitals. And how about sponsoring a poison-drink party for closer Christian fellowship?

While some use tongue-speaking to identify a fellow Christian, others use tongue-speaking to write off a fellow Christian. Some on both sides of the question are too quick with the reaction. As soon as the word is out that someone is speaking in tongues, some non-speakers want an immediate excommunication issued from the congregational leaders. Some claim that *all tongue-speaking is a work of the devil,* but this position cannot be definitively supported. Evidence strongly suggests that for some a psychosomatic source is the answer (See Stagg, Hinson, Oates, *Glossolalia,* Abingdon Press). It behooves us to look into some reasons, to recognize that needs of people in our churches are not being met, and then to begin to meet those needs! Isn't it easy for us to get so caught up in oiling the wheels of Christianity that we miss meeting some of the personal needs of the Christians? People are not just to be counted in our church programs; they are to count!

We all affirm that some uses of the physical tongue are definitively from the devil—slander, lying, gossip, backbiting, proud words, etc. It is interesting that we have not been as quick to ostracize these performers from the fellowship as we have the tongue-speakers. With slander, gossip, etc., we take seriously the Biblical teaching that a Christian grows into maturity; and if a brother is overtaken in a fault, we should seek to restore him in the spirit of gentleness and meekness (Gal. 6:1,2). Should we not be as patient with tongue-speakers? After all, tongue-speaking is surely no more divisive than slander, gossip, lies, etc. (Should we read Gal. 5:15 again?).

There is usually no need for an immediate heresy trial when a member in the congregation begins speaking in tongues. The act should not, however, be permitted to be displayed in public. Perhaps the first thing to share with the new tongue-speaker is the fact that Paul kept this kind of experience to himself (Notice in I Cor. 14:18 that Paul only lets us know about it when he needs to do so to correct a bad practice in Corinth, only when others are making too much of the experience).

The person who has begun speaking in tongues needs Christian fellowship as much as ever—if not more! The fact that he is now speaking in tongues *may be partly due to a need* for closer fellowship not being heretofore met. When a Christian brother begins to speak in tongues, other Christians should decide to love, care, understand, and share with him in activities which will result in mutual Christian growth. Speaking in tongues *per se* is not an open sin. It does not mean that the person doing it is no longer a child of God—nor does it mean that he *is* a child of God.

It is commendable that some people today are desiring a closer walk with God and are open to all they think God has for them. Perhaps the weakness of some of us is that *we do not care* what power is available to us and in us. Don't we all need to be reminded that our new birth *is* a birth of the Spirit and not just of water (John 3:5)? *The Holy Spirit* does *live within the Christian* (Rom. 8:9; I Cor. 6:19). We *have* become partakers of a divine nature (II Peter 1:4). The person of Christ *does* live within our earthly body (Gal. 3:27). The power of His resurrection *is available* to us (Rom. 6:5). *We do have divine power* with supernatural weapons to fight the cosmic spiritual battle in which we are engaged (II Cor. 10:3-5; Eph. 6:10ff). We *are* on a spiritual battleground with supernatural spiritual hosts against us (Eph. 6:11,12; I Peter 5:8; Rom. 8:38). In the gift of the Holy Spirit, *we have been given* the first installment of God's inheritance. That downpayment is God's guarantee that He will eventually grant to us His full inheritance. That Holy Spirit is a foretaste of the future. God's eternity has already invaded our temporalness (Eph. 1:13, 14; I Cor. 1:21; Eph. 4:30).

God's Holy Spirit is not just something to be discussed and debated, but instead is someone to be experienced. Is it possible that too many Christians have heard too little about the Holy Spirit, so that when we discover that He is available we expect some super-manifestation *because we haven't recognized Him earlier?*

He has been active, but we just have not given Him the credit. Isn't it time that our evangelistic preaching brings the

Holy Spirit into proper focus? If this had been done earlier, perhaps many of our present problems *would not have emerged!* Is it possible that we preach a plan and not a person, so that people know the proposition but not the person? Early Christians were concerned that people had the Holy Spirit (Acts 19:2) and not just that their sins were forgiven (Acts 2:38) at baptism! An over emphasis about the physical element—water, can overshadow the supraphysical element of the Spirit (I Cor. 12:12,13).

Both the tongue-speakers and the non-tongue-speakers can learn things from each other. Those who do not speak in tongues can learn from the apparent joy and devotional life of some who do. Those who do speak in tongues can learn from the practice of demanding a *"Thus saith the Lord"* from some of the non-speakers. All need to love (I Tim. 1:5). All need to be *actively* engaged in rightly dividing the Word of Truth (II Tim. 2:15). We all need to be involved in a personal witnessing program of evangelism. But we must keep the attitude of Apollos who, though his credentials were impressive, was still teachable (Acts 18:24-28). Both sides need to *study carefully* I Cor. 12:13ff which deals with attitudes.

Suggestions to Tongue-Speakers

If the Bible is the result of the Holy Spirit, then the Bible is a way to test the spirits. Tongue-speakers should study carefully I Cor. 13:8-10. The Bible book of *I Corinthians* outlines the 1st century regulations to tongue-speakers in that day. It is clearly anti-scriptural to practice speaking in tongues in violation of those regulations.

Tongue-speakers should not think that the Christian life is always lived on a mountain-top kind of experience. Jesus had his valleys. Paul had his. At one time Paul was distressed to the point of death (II Cor. 1:8). One thing which helped Paul was the support of fellow-Christians (II Cor. 2:13; I Thess. 3:1-8). God does not give us item for item what we request. He disciplines us through testing (II Cor. 12:8; James 1:2ff; I Peter 1:6ff; Rom. 5:3ff). Even Jesus needed suffering as a means to perfection (Heb. 2:10).

One primary witness to the gospel is our adorning of God's doctrine with personal Christian character (Titus 2:10). One should not get so hooked on an experience that he puts all of his Christian life into it. Remember Gal. 5:25, "If we live by the Spirit, *let us also walk by the Spirit."* That is in the context of the fruit of the Spirit (Gal. 5:22-24). The next verse begins to outline ways to walk by the Spirit: "Let us have no self-conceit, no provoking of one another, no envy of one another. . . ."

It is true that we are to be aglow with the Spirit (Rom. 12:11). But the way that *glow* is seen is discussed in Romans 12:9-21. The glow of the Spirit is seen when love is genuine, when we outdo one another in showing honor, when we are enthusiastic about God, when we serve the Lord we love, when we rejoice in hope, are patient in tribulation, constant in prayer, when we contribute to the needs of our brothers, when we don't retaliate, etc. The reason we know that is *the glow of the Spirit* is not only because of the context in Romans 12 but also because *that's the way Jesus lived;* and no one was more aglow with the Spirit than He. Perhaps the best initial advice to tongue-speakers is that they spend more time with the four Gospels, Romans, and I John, and less time with I Corinthians chapters 12-14.

Suggestions to Non-Tongue-Speakers

The non-tongue-speaker should feel neither inferior nor superior by the lack of the experience. Neither should he consider the tongue-speaking Christian to be an evil person just because he speaks in tongues. The non-speaker should seek to understand why the speaker desired the experience. Here are some attitudes which he may need to cultivate in his own life. (If these were more prominent in any congregation, the need for "a manifestation" of God would lessen.)

(1) A belief in prayer. Tongue-speaking Christians generally believe that God hears and answers prayer. Prayer is not usually *just a routine* for them. Should it be with us? Can't we pray for specific things? Do we need to put God into a box in which He hasn't placed Himself?

(2) More time with the Scriptures. Problems arise in churches when someone begins to practice tongues because many of the members do not know scriptural teaching. Many churches have become split because a new preacher taught a new, unscriptural doctrine—and no one knew how to challenge him. It is a slam to our hasty manner of electing church leaders when a new preacher can easily lead them to follow his teaching. Someone recently told me about the problems in his congregation and said, "None of us know enough Bible to do anything. By the time we study the issue (of tongues), the damage will have been done." When will we realize that a congregation *does not have to have elders, but a scriptural elder HAS to know the Bible!*

(3) A belief in the supernatural power of God. We must be careful that we do not try to keep the Holy Spirit locked up in a book. The Holy Spirit produced the Bible, but He does not live in the Bible—He lives in *people!* It is time that we see

and acknowledge the God who can heal and guide us. I am appalled that many Christians do not really *believe that God acts today.*

(4) Activity in witnessing. Part of the glossolalist's joy seems to come from witnessing. Shouldn't ours also? In the early church, both men and women *preached wherever they went* (Acts 8:1-4). The new Christian should be expected to witness immediately and should be told that the Holy Spirit is God's gift to him *partly to help him witness to others* about Jesus!

(5) Take down fake masks. We must die to public opinion and let the will of God shine through us. We should admit our faults to God (and if necessary, to others—Matt. 5:23,24; James 5:16), then accept the cleansing from God (I John 1:9).

(6) Know that we must grow. We cannot remain stagnant! Paul was very concerned about the growth of Christians he knew (see Gal. 4:19; Eph. 4:15; Col. 1:28,29; II Tim. 1:5).

Suggestions to Every Christian

Perhaps the best way to prevent a crisis in the local church over this issue is to work at a closer, loving fellowship and to engage in an in-depth study of the subject of the Holy Spirit. It serves little purpose to ignore a topic until it becomes a problem. We should not suppose that we can ignore an issue and it will not come up in our congregation.

The congregation should study the nature and purpose of the church (biblically, not traditionally), the nature and purpose of the Holy Spirit, the nature and purpose of Christian unity and fellowship, and the nature and purpose of "tongues" in the 1st century. Many Christians today know less about the Holy Spirit of God than about any other reality. The tragedy is the lack of knowledge that the Holy Spirit *lives inside each Christian!* The congregation as a whole should also think out the Biblical way to handle diversity. *What should the congregation do* when a brother is overtaken in a fault (Gal.6:1,2)?

The congregation should study the characteristics of love. As spiritual gifts without love *are no good* (I Cor. 13:1-4), neither is truth without love any good. People will not accept the truth we proclaim if they cannot stand our attitude, so truth must be spoken in love (Eph. 4:15a). The person who presents truth with an "I know it all" attitude places himself above the attitude with which Jesus taught. *Whatever our position is on this issue,* we must admit that each of us is fallible, and thus each should remain open to the teaching of the Bible. It is not our task to deny experiences, but rather to understand them as God does.

The testimonies of many tongue-speakers suggest that they experience a closer kind of fellowship with other Christians after the experience. This may be because fellow tongue-speakers share an identity in this gift, and rejoice in that mutuality. I have been to Pentecostal meetings in which people asked others, *"Have you received the gift?"* When the answer was *yes*, there was mutual joy expressed. Is it possible that we often do not have that kind of fellowship centered around the person of Christ who lives in each Christian (Gal. 3:27)? We who teach that the Holy Spirit comes into a person who has expressed faith, repentance, and baptism often show a "so what" attitude when we hear that someone has been immersed. We give the idea that we may be thinking, *"I wonder if it will last"* or *"I wonder how much emotion was used."* If becoming a Christian *is* the most significant act a person has done up to that time in his life, we ought to communicate that significance. If we have become united in Christ, we ought to recognize it and then live it! If Christ does live in each new Christian, shouldn't we rejoice in it immediately? Mutual fellowship is a necessity for complete joy (I John 1: 1-4). It seems cruel for a newly-baptized person to walk out of the dressing room to see the backs of his new brothers and sisters hurrying off to a roast beef dinner! *That's the time for a Christian party!* We need to teach the identity which every Christian shares—that identity *is the Holy Spirit.* Let us together praise God for Him!

Meeting the essential needs of a new Christian is the best way to have a trouble-free church. The need of a new Christian babe is the same as a new physical babe. The first need is love and fellowship. But often we do not immediately fellowship the new Christian into the social life of other Christians. We continue as if each should stay in the same sphere he was in before the new Christian was converted. The life of every Christian should change somewhat *the moment another person is added* to the congregation. His fellowship cannot be done just at the gathering hour; although it *is* to be done there, for our gatherings are to help one another (Heb. 10:24,25).

The second need of a new babe is for nourishment. As we do not give steak to a new-born physical babe, so we should not expect a new spiritual babe to digest the same lessons that a Christian of 50 years is digesting. We need to rethink the initial education of new Christians. He should get milk before meat (I Peter 2:1-3).

There is a third initial need that when met will help ward

off a desire for special manifestation—that is the need to be used. We should use the members in their suffering servant role. The greatest blessings which come to Christians come *through their service.* We must return to the pattern of the church as seen in Eph. 4:11-16. Each Christian has *charisma* to be used for the total Body of Christ. It is as each Christian is *being used* that both he and the church are nourished properly. The congregation must provide the environment in which the new Christian can get fellowship, nourishment and service. The church probably has the richest untapped abilities of any earthly group.

But there remains the perplexing problem of what to do if tongue-speaking begins in a non-tongue-speaking congregation. Let us not fly off the handle. Let us realize that *people* are involved—yea, *God's* people—our brothers and sisters. Let us not isolate ourselves from them. That will drive them to those who will fellowship with them—other glossolalists. Let us teach and live what it means to be *aglow with the Spirit.* Above all, let us relate to those Christians who differ with us with the characteristics of a Christian (see Rom. 12:10ff; Eph. 4:25ff; Col. 3:12ff—"be tenderly affectioned one to another; in honor preferring one another" "Let all bitterness, and wrath, and anger, and clamor, and railing, be put away from you, with all malice" "Put on . . . a heart of compassion, kindness, lowliness, meekness, longsuffering; forbearing one another, and forgiving each other . . .").

An informed, loving fellowship is the best way to ward off trouble. It is also the best environment in which to handle trouble after it begins. Let us seek to understand why a person is speaking in tongues, and then let Christ minister to him through us. We should engage in a careful study of the texts and logic being used by the person. But, remember, the attitude of the teaching will speak louder at first than the action of the teaching.

However, if the person is not teachable and insists on teaching and practicing his tongue-speaking *in a way that will be divisive for the congregation,* then the advice of Titus 3:10 should be heeded. But remember that the factious person can be either the tongue-speaker *or the non-tongue-speaker.* The *reaction* can be as wrong scripturally as the *action.* The testing may soon come to your congregation. It may come partly to mature it. *Are you ready?*

DISCUSSION QUESTIONS

1. Why cannot special experiences be used to recognize a person as a Christian?
    a. Relate this to lesson 1.
    b. Relate this to I Corinthians 12.
2. What should be the reaction toward a tongue-speaker?
3. What should the reaction not be?
4. What does it mean to be aglow with the Spirit?
5. How do you know when a person is aglow with the Spirit? Relate this to Galatians 5:22, 23.
6. What can tongue speakers and non-tongue speakers learn from each other?
7. What are good measures for a congregation to take to prevent difficulty over tongues?

3

AN IN-DEPTH LOOK AT THE "PERFECT" OF I CORINTHIANS 13

I Corinthians 13:8-13 is one of the toughest sections in the Corinthian correspondences—especially as read in English translations. Some teachings are clear: (1) love is permanent, and (2) tongues, knowledge, and prophecy are temporary. But some questions arise—

1) What is the knowledge and prophecy of verse 9? (Will knowledge *per se* ever pass away?)
2) What is "the perfect" in verse 10?
3) What does "imperfect" mean in verses 9 and 10?
4) What does it mean in verse 12 to "understand fully"?

It is my hope that this lesson will not muddy the water more, but will help clear it. It is my intention to look at this passage as objectively as I can. I am not interested in perpetuating any traditions which are not scriptural. As a matter of fact, I prefer to *shatter traditions*. I am not interested in feeding a "party-line." I want to understand my idea of the truth by the text and not strive to understand the text by my idea of truth.

Now let's dig deeply into I Corinthians 13:8-13. In verse 8, the permanency of love is spotlighted, *"Love never ends."* The next phrase in the Greek begins with a little word which introduces a contrast *(de)* and is translated *but*. This introduces a contrast between the permanency of love just announced, and the transitory nature of three other phenomena. However, a very interesting thing occurs—two different words are used to describe the temporary nature of the three, putting them into two different categories! Prophecies and knowledge are considered together, while tongues (foreign languages—see lesson 5) is put into another category.

The word used with prophecies and knowledge is a word that refers to the setting aside of one thing when something else comes *(katargeo)*. This is the connotation of the word in every other place Paul uses it in the Corinthian correspondence (I Cor. 1:28; 2:6; 6:13; 13:14; 15:24,26; II Cor. 3:7, 11,13,14; Gal. 3:17 *[negative usage here];* Eph. 2:15; II Tim. 1:10; Rom. 7:2,6).

Paul's use of this word indicates that knowledge and prophecies will give way to something else, i.e., they will be replaced or superseded. In a sense, they will be absorbed into something better, rather than cease altogether. The word which describes the temporary nature of tongues is not the same, but is a word that means *stop*. There will be no replacing. The tongues will cease when the knowledge and prophecies give way to something better.

But why will they give way to something better—and when? Verse 9 answers the *why?* and verse 10 the *when?*

Why Something Better?

We cannot understand verse 10 without first taking a careful look at verse 9, because of the three possible meanings of the word translated *perfect.* That Greek word *(teleios)* can mean:

1) Something without a flaw, *perfect,* or
2) Something entirely together, *whole,* or
3) Something which has reached its goal, *complete.*

Now which is the translation in verse 10? Verse 9 gives us the clue, but that clue is hidden in the RSV rendering.

Verse 9 begins with a very important word, "for" (*gar*). This is a transition word which introduces an explanation or a reason for a preceding statement. *[By the way, not enough writers take seriously the implications of the transition words in Greek.]* Verse 9 GIVES THE REASON for saying that prophecies and knowledge will be replaced. The literal translation is this—*"For we are (now) knowing from a part (a piece at a time) and we are (now) prophesying from a part."* The RSV rendering that "our knowledge is imperfect and our prophecy is imperfect" is too ambiguous and is not helpful. First, the main words are verbs and not nouns. Secondly, the word *imperfect* is too frequently misunderstood. The RSV *imperfect* comes from two Greek words which literally mean "out of a part" *(ek merous).* The New Testament usually uses the phrase "out of a part *(ek merous)* or "from a part" *(apo merous)* to refer to a state of imcompletion—a partial situation which needs wholeness

(Rom. 11:25; 15:15,24; II Cor. 1:14; 2:5).

Paul was saying that the knowing and prophesying of verse 8 will be set aside because as a source *(ek)* of revelation, they are piecemeal. A better source was to come—a complete source. The gifts of prophecy and inspired knowledge produced only limited pieces of divine revelation. The whole revelation of God's will was to come, so that a complete knowledge would be unnecessary.

We should note that in verse 9, Paul did not mention tongues. He did not need to explain why they would give way to something better, because they were not going to be replaced when the need for them had passed.

When Does It Come?

When would that something better come? Verse 10 tells us. Verse 10 begins with that very important transition word *(de)* which introduces a contrast. While verse 9 speaks about the piecemeal source *(out of a part)* for knowledge and speech, verse 10 by contrast introduces a source where the missing pieces are put together, a complete source. Verse 10 should read this way—*"But when the whole [thing] comes, the [thing] out of a part will be set aside."* This is the literal translation from the Greek. Note that again the phrase "out of a part" *(ek merous)* appears in verse 10 as well as in verse 9. This phrase is translated in the RSV as *imperfect*. The word *perfect* stands in direct contrast with the words *out of a part (piece)*. So, within a context of "source" the only proper way the word *perfect* in verse 10 can be rendered is *whole or complete* (instead of *perfect*). It is here the opposite of partial. It means *whole*.

Then what is the whole or complete thing of verse 10? It

is the "put-together pieces" spoken of in verse 9.

During the early days of the church, God gave to various persons special gifts for the purpose of equipping His church. Among these gifts were knowledge and prophecies. Knowledge and prophecies in I Corinthians 13 clearly refer to that knowledge and speech *directly inspired by God.* The early church was built upon men having such gifts (see Ephesians 2:20). These gifts were given to curb subjectivity. Many people were claiming to have a word from God. To curb the ambiguity of so many "voices" claiming inspiration, God inspired some and gave to others the ability to discern His Spirit. We do not know all the dynamics about this.

All Parts Fit Together

However, we do know this: Each man received just a *part* of God's total revelation. God gave to one man *this* particular word and to another man *that* particular word. Paul recognized that the inspired knowledge and speaking of selected individuals was partial—a word from God here, and a word from God there. Would this partial revelation go on forever? Paul says, "No." *There will be a time when the pieces (out of a part,* ek merous) *will be put together!* And when that happens, men will get their knowledge and speech about God's revelation from the whole *(teleios)* because the parts will have been absorbed into the whole. Therefore, the inspired knowledge and prophecy of verse 8 which is from a partial source (verse 9) will give way (be set aside) when a better source comes—the whole, the perfect (verse 10). Note again that this passage indicates that tongues will simply cease. As a matter of fact, church history shows that tongues largely did cease even before the writing of the New Testament was entirely finished.

It is my understanding that the *perfect of verse 10 can* most easily refer to the completed "mystery" of God. Paul speaks often of God's revelation as a *mystery*. That was a military word of the first century which meant the overall strategy of a general. Here's the way it was used: Before a battle, a general would call in his leaders and give to each one a different order. Each then had *a piece of* the total strategy. Each would pass this on to the men of his charge who were to fulfill it. Often this was done without necessarily knowing that *other pieces* were in existence. Men under different leaders were getting different pieces depending upon their situation. After the battle was won, the general would call all his leaders together and explain to them the pieces of his battle plan so that each saw *the total strategy.*

This combination of *pieces put together* was called "mystery" (*musterion*). The role of God's church is to let all men see the total (put together) plan of God's *musterion* (Eph. 3:9, 10). Before God's new plan was put together, it existed in pieces because He, like a general, gave certain pieces to various men who passed them on to the people of their charge. But later the Commander-in-chief caused all the pieces to be put together! That strategy (*musterion*) is our New Testament.

The Completed Whole

When the whole comes, the parts are absorbed *into the whole* like a child is changed into the adult (verse 11). To see the whole is to see how all the parts interrelate. It is to see the outline *and details* clearly. That's what Paul is saying in verse 12. *"We now see in a mirror dimly, but then face to face."* He explains his meaning in the next sentence, which parallels exactly. That is, *I see in a mirror dimly* equals *I now know out of a part* (ek merous), and *then face to face* equals *understand fully*.

"Face to face" does not require us to think of standing in the Lord's presence after the resurrection of the saints. It may be only a vivid expression of the wholeness and clarity of revelation which would be available after the completed Word of God made prophesying unnecessary. Remember how God spoke to Moses *"face to face"* (Exodus 33:11). Yet when Moses asked to see God, he was told, *"Thou canst not see my face; for man shall not see me and live"* (Exodus 33:17-20). We often do not realize how full and intimate a knowledge of God has been given to us in His word. Consider John 15:15; 16:12-15; II Peter 1:3; II Tim.3:14-17.

The reference to a mirror refers to a partial look, i.e., not a clear look. The outline may be seen, but not any clear details. In the first century, the only mirrors available were polished metal. But polished metal never allowed as clear or full a view as looking directly with the eyes. So the term "look into a mirror" was commonly used to refer to partial knowledge (Philo uses it to refer to man's partial knowledge of God). It is also important to note that the word *mirror* is used elsewhere in the New Testament to refer to a look at the revelation of God (see James 1:23-25; II Cor.3:18). Since the metaphor *mirror* was used in the first century to refer to our partial knowledge of God and is elsewhere used to refer to looking at the revelation from God, we should so consider it in this passage. Before the pieces of God's new revelation were put together, our look at it did not reveal all the details; but when *the pieces were put together,* we could see His revelation *face to face.* This is a way to speak of seeing something clearly—to see from a correct or holistic perspective so that both outline and details can be seen. This is further clarified in the next sentence, "then I shall know fully." In the context, this means *to know the total strategy of God.* As the leaders came to know fully the general's plan after he put all the pieces together for them, *so we can know God's completed plan!*

Verse 13 gives us a clincher—*"Faith, hope, and love abide."* These will abide after the *perfect* has come. Thus the perfect in verse 10 cannot refer to the second coming because when that happens, our faith will be turned into sight and our hope into reality. The gender of "perfect" (*teleios*) in verse 10 is neuter *(teleion).* To suggest that Paul would use this form of the word to speak of his Lord is very unsatisfactory. That would depersonalize Jesus. In fact, Paul is fond of speaking of Jesus and God; and especially so in this letter. He refers to Them directly at least 20 times in the first 9 verses of I Corinthians, and he knows how to speak about the 2nd coming in a clear way (1:7)! God is called *perfect* in Matthew 5:48, but the gender is masculine. To change the gender from masculine to neuter is to say "a perfect *thing"* instead of a perfect person. Every other time this word appears in the New Testament in the neuter gender, it refers to a non-personal thing, and twice it is used to refer to the will or law of God (Rom. 12:2; James 1:25). Thus it is not unusual for God's revelation to be called *perfect (teleion).*

The *perfect* in verse 10 in its present context seems to refer to God's *completed revelation* which had come from pieces to men here and there, but was later put together into a whole. When that happens, the piecemeal source for inspired knowledge and prophecy will have been set aside by being absorbed into the whole. To understand *perfect* in another way is to say that inspired knowledge and prophecies from pieces *(ek merous)* are valid in the church today. That would mean that *we have no absolute, completed revelation from God.* Church history reveals that the church in the early centuries rejected that kind of thinking. They stood upon the completion and finality of the canon at the cost of their lives.

What about tongues? They merely stop—thus, not as significant as knowledge and prophecy. This is not to deny the power of God, but rather to accept the strategy God has outlined to make His power known to all generations for all time. But we cannot glean from this chapter *when* tongues will cease. The coming of the perfect relates to the ceasing of inspired knowledge and prophecy, not to the ceasing of tongues. Tongue-speaking could cease before or after the perfect comes. The verse says that which is "in part" will cease when the perfect comes—only knowledge and prophecy are said to be "in part".

Both sides of the tongue-speaking question are in error in using this chapter to either prove their early discontinuance or their continuation until the Second Coming. We must consider the nature and purpose of tongues in evaluating their longevity, not the identification of the "perfect."

DISCUSSION QUESTIONS

1. What three things will cease when the perfect comes?
2. What possible meanings can the word **perfect** have?

3. What helps us decide what it means in I Cor. 13:10?

4. Discuss why, if the **perfect** refers to the second coming of Jesus—

    a. Why are the other gifts in I Cor. 12:4-10 and 12:28-30 not mentioned. Will they be needed after Jesus comes?

    b. Why was the Bible written if directly-inspired knowledge and preaching would always be with us?

    c. Why didn't Paul clearly say he meant the second coming of Christ?

5. Why would a completed Bible absorb inspired knowledge and prophecy?

NOTE: It is quite possible that **teleios** (perfect) refers to the mature individual. That seems to be its usage elsewhere in I Cor. and its most common usage elsewhere in the New Testament. If this be the case, Paul is saying that when a Christian reaches maturity, he will not need the inspired knowledge and prophecy of individuals, for he will have incorporated them into himself (but not tongues). We are to use our individual charisma for that purpose (Eph. 4:11-16, especially the use of "perfect"—there translated **mature**, in v. 13).

4

AN IN-DEPTH LOOK AT "KNOW FULLY" IN I COR. 13:12

One of the arguments used to support tongue-speaking by Christians today is to say that the *perfect* in I Cor. 13:8 refers to the second coming of Jesus. One reason for this position is the appearance of the word translated *know fully* in verse 12. The thought is that the phrase means *to entirely understand all things* and since that cannot happen in this life, the *perfect* must refer to the second coming of Jesus.

The New American Standard Bible translates I Cor. 13:12 as, "For now we see in a mirror dimly, but then face to face; Now I know in part, but then I shall know fully just as I also have been known."

What does it mean to "know fully"? The word translated "know fully" is *epiginosko*. This is a compound of the verb *ginosko* and the prefix *epi*. *Ginosko* simply means *know*. It is the most common word-root for the verb *know* and the noun *knowledge* in the Bible. The difference between this common word and the word used in I Cor. 13:12 is a prepositional prefix *epi* which, when used alone, means *upon*. [When a preposition is prefixed to a Greek verb, it sometimes intensifies the action of that verb.] Our task here is to do an inductive study of the compound *epiginosko* to determine what it means. Does it have a different meaning than the simple *ginosko?*

To take the position that the compound *epiginosko* means to "know everything" or to know something "fully" is to suggest that this word could not have a common usage in this life. However, it was a very commonly used word in the Greek Old Testament, in the New Testament, and in non-Christian literature such as Philo. The compound verb is used at least 80 times in the Old Testament and 40 times in the New Testament, not counting the numerous times the noun form is used.

What do we discover in those usages? We discover that the word is used *interchangeably* with the simple form *ginosko*. Bultmann, in his article on *ginosko* in *The Theological Dictionary of the New Testament* rightly observes that in early Christian writing there is no distinction between the simple and compound verbs of *ginosko—they are synonymous!*

Below are some references which reveal the interchangeable usage. Note that in both cases the word is translated merely, "know, acknowledge, recognize, etc.", rather than to "know fully" or know everything.

AN IN-DEPTH LOOK AT "KNOW FULLY"

ginosko, used in—	*epiginosko,* used in—
Rom. 1:21	Rom. 1:28
Rom. 7:7; 15:14	Rom. 3:20
Mark 8:17	Mark 2:8
Luke 24:35	Luke 24:31
II Cor. 8:9	Col. 1:16
Rom. 2:18	Rom. 1:32

The interchangeableness of these two words is even more clearly seen in the parallels of the Gospels. While one account will have *ginosko,* its parallel in a companion Gospel will have *epiginosko* (that is no problem since both words meant exactly the same thing in the 1st century). Below are listed some Gospel parallels:

ginosko, used in—	*epiginosko,* used in—
Luke 8:46	Mark 5:30
Luke 6:44	Matt. 7:16
Luke 9:11	Mark 6:33
Luke 10:22	Matt. 11:27

Paul himself used the word *epiginosko* (the compound, as used in I Cor. 13:12) 26 different times in either the noun or verb forms. In *I Corinthians,* he used it 3 different times—in 13:12; 14:37; and 16:18. As used in chapters 14 and 16, it certainly doesn't mean to "know everything." It simply means to know, recognize or acknowledge. Any one of those renderings would be a better translation for *epiginosko* in I Cor. 13:12 than "know fully," which is misleading to those who do not know the Greek.

When Paul wants to speak of "full" knowledge, he knows that he must add something to the word *epiginosko* and he does in II Cor. 1:13. There he adds the word which means *complete* or *completely—telous*. That text is correctly translated *"know fully."* But *telous* does not appear in I Cor. 13:12.

To take the position that *epiginosko* is the kind of knowledge that cannot happen in this life (i.e., it is complete and we must wait until heaven for it) is erroneous. Paul himself uses the same word he uses in I Cor. 13:12 to speak of knowledge to be obtained or that is already obtained *in this life*. Below is a list of things to know in this life where the word *epiginosko* is used in the Greek text. In none of these cases does it mean, "know fully," "know completely," or "know everything."

1. The will of God—Romans 1:32
2. His writings—I Cor. 14:37.
3. People—I Cor. 16:18; II Cor. 6:9.
4. Self—II Cor. 13:5 (in fact, Paul *demands* here that we know [*epiginosko*] self).
5. Grace of God—Col. 1:6 (this has already been obtained in Colosse).
6. The truth—I Tim. 4:3; 2:4; II Tim.2:25; 3:7; Titus 1:1; Heb. 10:26 (Paul makes it clear that knowledge of the truth [*epiginosis*] is a MUST in this life—it is not something available only in the next life).
7. God—Rom. 1:38; 10:2 (to not know [*epiginosko*] God in this life is damnation, he says). Also Eph. 1:17; Phil. 1:9; Col. 1:10 (to know God to the *epiginosko* degree is obviously possible *in this life!*).
8. Sin—Romans 3:20.
9. God's will—Colossians 1:9.
10. God's mystery—Colossians 2:2.

AN IN-DEPTH LOOK AT "KNOW FULLY"

11. Every good thing—Philemon 6.
12. We are to be renewed in this life in *epiginosko* kind of knowledge—Colossians 3:10.
13. Peter speaks of a present *epiginosko* kind of knowledge of Christ—II Peter 1:3, 8; 2:20.

These usages suggest that the word in I Cor. 13:12 does *not* refer to something to be obtained only in heaven. It is a common word to refer to knowledge which can be obtained here on earth (check out its 80 usages in the Greek Old Testament also). The translation of *epiginosko* in I Cor. 13:12 as "know fully" is misleading. To my knowledge, the word is *never* translated that way anywhere else in the Bible or in other Greek literature!

Epiginosko in this context means no more than to know (*ginosko*) God's revelation in its completed form. This understanding comes from the context however, rather than from the word itself. In this passage, *epiginosko* does not mean to know *everything* fully. Nor does it mean to know *anything* fully!

To suggest that the compound *epiginosko* is more full or complete knowledge than the simple *ginosko* is to overlook the additional fact that the simple form is the *normal* word used to speak about the knowledge that Jesus and God have. For examples, see Matt. 6:3; 7:23; 10;26; 12:15; 15:33; John 2:24; 8:55; 10:15; plus hundreds of other places—the Gospels are full of them. *Ginosko* is used hundreds of times referring to God's knowledge (which is a complete kind of knowledge compared to what we now know), while *epiginosko* is used to refer to His knowledge only a few times.

Those who suggest that *epiginosko* in I Cor. 13:12 is

complete knowledge like God's have little objective evidence for their position. Most evidence points the other way. There is no linguistic support and even less theological support for suggesting that man will ever have complete knowledge of all things as God does. That would be to do away with the eternal qualitative and quantitative difference between God and His creatures. Why need God in heaven if we will there have His complete knowledge of everything? That temptation got the first people into trouble in Eden (Gen. 3:5). In eternity, I expect to continue to be a creature of God—made in His image, but still less than He. I shall praise, honor, and glorify the only One who has complete knowledge—forever and ever (that the angels do not have complete knowledge is clear from I Peter 1:12).

Bultmann points out that *ginosko* was understood by the Greeks to refer to the kind of knowledge an adult has over against what a child knows. This fits the idea in I Cor. 13:11 well. Our context seems to be discussing a knowledge which has a complete source—not piece-meal.

Paul used a good illustration for that century. To look into a polished metal (1st century mirrors were polished metal instead of silvered glass) was to not see in proper perspective. It was to see as a child sees. This is compared to looking at God's revelation from the piecemeal sources from which revelation was coming at that time. But when the completion is done, then we can look to His revelation and see it as it fully is. That's like seeing the face as it is directly, face-to-face. It must be mentioned here that to see the face from a face-to-face look is not yet to see the self completely. There's still part of the real me that cannot be seen in any mirror.

I cannot find that I Cor. 13:12 suggests a complete or full

knowledge which cannot be obtained in this life. It does not negate the position that the *perfect* in I Cor. 13:10 refers to the completed Scriptures, the coming of which will absorb inspired prophecy and knowledge and cause God-given tongue-speaking to cease.

DISCUSSION QUESTIONS

1. What does the term **know fully** in I Cor. 13:12 mean in the Greek? Support your answer.
2. What is it that we are to know in I Cor. 13:12?
3. How do we know it?
4. What relationship does this have with that which is perfect?

5

AN IN-DEPTH LOOK AT "TONGUES" IN THE BIBLE

Much has been written on the subject of tongues in the New Testament; however, few writers deal with the most elementary research—the meaning and use of the Greek word translated into the English as *tongue* or *tongues*. The Greek word for *tongue* is *glossa,* from which we derive our word *glossolalia. Glossolalia* comes from two Greek words—*glossa,* tongue, and *lalia,* speaking.

Literally, *glossolalia* means *tongue-speaking.* But just what is tongue-speaking? To answer that question, we must determine how the word *glossa* is used in the Bible. The objective methodology for this is to research its every appearance in the Bible. A research of every usage of the word *glossa* in the Greek Bible reveals:

IN THE OLD TESTAMENT

The word *glossa* is used in the Greek O. T. no less than 100 times. It is used in one of two ways—

(1) As the physical member in our mouths. See such places as Joshua 10:21; Judges 7:5,6; Job 5:21; 6:30; 20:12, 16; 29:10; 33:2; Psalm 5:9; Proverbs 10:20 (many others in Proverbs also); Isaiah 33:6; 41:7.

(2) As a known language of a known people. See such places as Gen. 10:5, 20, 31; 11:7; Nehemiah 13:24; Jeremiah 5:15; Ezekiel 3:6; Isaiah 3:8; 19:18; 66:18; 28:11 *(this use is very significant because Paul refers to it in I Cor. 14:21).*

The use of glossa is so closely connected with a known language that at times it sounds as if it is used in apposition with *nation* or *foreign people* in the same sentence (see Jeremiah 18:8; Daniel 3:4, 29; 6:25).

Someone may suggest that Zephaniah 3:9 is an exception to the two usages above. The text reads in the *Revised Standard Version,* "Yea, at that time I will change the speech of the peoples to a pure speech. . . ." Some may suggest that this refers to a heavenly kind of speech; however, the context negates that idea, because verse 13 explains what is meant by *pure speech.* It reads, ". . . nor shall there be found in their mouth *a deceitful tongue.* . . ."

Not once in the O. T. is the Greek word *glossa* used to refer to an ecstatic or supra-human language. Every time it is used, it should be translated as either (1) tongue—what we have in our mouth, or (2) language.

IN THE NEW TESTAMENT

The word *glossa* is used no less than fifty times in the New Testament. At this point, we will not consider the six usages in Acts and the nineteen usages in I Corinthians. The objective research of the usages elsewhere will give us a clue to the expected usages in those two books.

In the N. T., *glossa* is also used in one of two ways: (1) As the physical member in our mouths. See Mark 7:33, 35; Luke 1:64; 16:24; Rom. 3:13; 14:11; Phil. 2:11; James 1:26; 3:5, 6, 8; I Peter 3:10; Rev. 16:10. (2) As a known language. See I John 3:18; Rev. 5:9 (The new song here is knowable content in a common language). The usage in the New Testament is also so closely connected with a known language that at times it sounds as if it is being used appositionally with *nation* or *foreign people* in the same sentence. See Rev. 7:9; 10:11; 11:9; 13:7; 14:6; 17:15. Outside of Acts and I Corinthians, the word *glossa* is not used to refer to an ecstatic or supra-human language. That thought is foreign to Biblical thinking thus far in our study.

Now we must ask, "What does *glossa* mean in Acts and in I Corinthians?" Based upon research thus far, it would be expected that the word would be used as it is in every other Bible verse.

Luke's first usage in Acts is in chapter 2. There it is clear that *glossa* is used as a known foreign language (verses 3, 4, 11, 26). In verse 8, the Greek word *dialektos* (from which we get our English word "dialect," and which always means a language of a nation), is used interchangeably with *glossa* found in verse 11. That interchangeable usage is very significant to note—it tells us how Luke understands *glossa!*

dialektos	*glossa*
(dialect, language)	(tongue, language)
verse 8—"And how is it that we hear each of us in his own *dialektos*"	verse 11—"We hear them telling in our own *glossa*"

Peter explained this as a fulfillment of Joel 2:28, which is a prophecy that looks to the advent of a new age. Peter makes it clear that the sign that God's new age had come was the use of foreign languages—not ecstatic utterances. Note that ecstatic utterances would hardly have been a sign because many pagan religions were practicing that in the 1st century—e.g., Dionysius, Bacides, Cybele, etc. There are records of ecstatic utterances being practiced by pagans as early as the 15th century before Christ. Men on the birthdate of Christ's Church would not have been amazed to hear ecstatic utterances. These were common! Today, ecstatic utterances are still common among primitive pagan religions (see *The Greeks and the Irrational* by E. R. Dodds and *Possessions* by T. K. Oesterreich).

What does *glossa* mean elsewhere in Acts? It is used in only two other verses—10:46 and 19:6. The usage in 10:46 is the same as in Acts 2, as explained by Peter in 11:17. He says it is the same *(equal* in Greek) gift. There is no reason to suspect that Luke changed his usage in 19:6. We have already seen that he considers the usage to be synonymous with *dialektos* (Acts 2:8).

Now how is *glossa* used in I Corinthians? From a usage analysis elsewhere in the Bible, we would expect one of two usages—(1) physical tongue in the mouth, or (2) a foreign language. If we had no presuppositions, this is the methodology we would follow. If this methodology had been followed by all, many misleading ideas would not have "gotten off the ground."

The word *unknown* which appears in some versions is not in the original Greek. Its addition to the English text has no textual support. Until I Corinthians, the Bible does not speak about any "unknown" *glossa*. In fact, I Cor. 12:10 and 28 say that there are "various kinds of tongues." The word *kind* refers to a family or genealogy; Paul could not know that one was from a different family than another if they had actually been *unknown* languages.

The phrase "There are various *kinds*" is significant. The Greek word translated "various" is *heteros,* which means "different." Every time this word is used in conjunction with *glossa,* it refers to a known foreign language. *This is the construction in* Acts 2:4 *and in* I Cor. 14:21. The latter is a quote from Isaiah 28:11, which is a reference to the Assyrian language. When Luke used *heteros* and *glossa* together, he referred to *a foreign language.*

Paul and Luke travelled together. It is unlikely that Paul would use the same construction to refer to a different phenomenon than Luke had in mind. It is further unlikely that Paul would use an O. T. reference which speaks about a known foreign language to discuss an ecstatic utterance in an *unknown* language (I Cor. 14:21 and Isaiah 28:11).

There is one other important fact to consider in determining the nature of the tongues mentioned in I Cor. 14. That is the meaning of the word *interpret* or *interpretation.* The Greek word is *hermeneuo,* from which we get our English word *Hermeneutics.* In one form or another, that word is used 13 times in the New Testament. What does it mean?

Outside I Corinthians, it is used to mean *to translate* words from one known language into another known language. See John 1:38, 42; 9:7; Heb. 7:2; Acts 9:36. The only exception to this is in Luke 24:27. There it is used to mean *to explain* the content-meaning from one known language *into the same known language.* Never is the word used in the Bible to mean to interpret an unknown language into a known language!

The word *hermeneuo* used with *glossa* enhances the position that Paul's subject in I Cor. 14 is a known foreign language which is translatable. Thus its nature could be checked out by many who knew the language. It is further noted that the word *glossa* referred to a *known* language. It was not used to speak about some language which had not been discovered, or which was being used in isolation. The languages mentioned were in common usage. There was no guessing or extensive linguistic analysis done to determine its nature.

The above facts suggest that except when *glossa* is referring to the physical member in the mouth, it should be translated as "language" for the sake of clarity. Some may question this thesis on the basis of I Cor. 13:1, which speaks of tongues of angels; however, we read too much *into* the text to suppose that it suggests that angels have a language all their own. Angels are God's messengers. From the evidence we have, God has always communicated to man in man's own language.

I Cor. 13:1 uses the same kind of argument Paul used in Galatians 1:8. It is a way to say, "It doesn't matter *who* is speaking or preaching." To suggest that angels have their own special language which is better than any of ours (as the meaning of I Cor. 13:1) is to say that they also must have their own special gospel which is worse than ours (as the meaning of the parallel passage, Gal. 1:8).

It is an interesting paradox that many of those who say that "tongues" is a heavenly language usually also say the "perfect" in I Cor. 13:10 refers to the Second Coming, at which time the "heavenly language" will cease—just as men are victoriously ushered into heaven itself!

It is very important that our communication to any person be understandable. After all, that's what God did in Jesus. And that's what God caused to happen on the day of Pentecost when the church was born. It is by understandable preaching that men are brought to faith (Romans 10). Therefore, let us preach God's Word and live it in love. Let us seek to communicate as Jesus did, both in our praying and in our preaching. I would rather imitate Him who is called Christ than those of the Corinthian church who are called carnal (I Cor. 3:1-4). Wouldn't you?

DISCUSSION QUESTIONS

1. What does **glossa** mean in the O.T.? In the New?
2. What does it mean in Acts 2? Support your answer from the context in Acts 2.
3. In connection with **tongue** in I Cor. 14,
    a) What is misleading about the word **unknown** which appears in some versions?
    b) Relate the nature of these tongues to Isaiah 28 as recorded in I Corinthians 14:21.
4. What does **interpret** mean and how does this help to know the nature of tongues?
5. What does the phrase **tongues of angels** mean in 13:1?

6

A LOOK AT I CORINTHIANS 14
IN ITS LITERARY CONTEXT

The situation in the church at Corinth could be described in one word as *sectarian*. Although Paul affirms that God called Christians in Corinth into one fellowship (1:10), they were living in factions (1:12). Many problems troubled their fellowship:

1. Cliques were formed and maintained (1:12; 3:3, 4).

2. Different sources for knowledge and authority were accepted and demanded (1:22).

3. Jealousies and strife were common (3:3).

4. Different values were placed upon necessary functions (3:5-15).

5. Immorality among the members was permitted (5:1-8; 6:1-8).

6. Intra-member lawsuits were carried out (6:1-8).

73

7. Misunderstandings about marriage seemed common (chapter 7).

8. Disagreements over certain ethical decisions appear to be sharp (chapter 8; 10:23-33).

9. Some were participating in demon worship (10:14-22).

10. Some women were being improper in worship (11:1-16; 14:34-36).

11. Conduct during the Lord's Supper (the Communion) was improper—so improper that the service harmed rather then helped the fellowship (11:17-23).

12. There was misunderstanding about spiritual gifts (chapters 12 through 14).

13. Some even began to doubt the resurrection of the dead (chapter 15).

Attitudes which fed these problems were primarily selfishness, jealousy, and pride. Note that Paul uses the word for *arrogant* or *puffed up* seven times in all of his writings, and six of those uses are in this one letter—4:6, 18, 29; 5:2; 8:1; 13:4.

One of the major problems in the congregation is their misunderstanding of spiritual gifts, particularly the use of God's gift of tongues. Paul devotes 3 chapters in I Cor. to this problem (12, 13 and 14). Chapters 12 and 13 lay the groundwork for chapter 14. Without a careful study of chapters 12 and 13, the significance of chapter 14 can be easily missed. One might wonder why Paul devotes more attention to this problem than to the people's doubt about the resurrection, or to their sexual immorality, their intra-membership lawsuits, or to their party splits. However, the issue of their misuse of tongues may not be divorced from these other issues!

A LOOK AT I CORINTHIANS 14

What is the link between the misuse of spiritual gifts and these other problems? If one is convinced that his *specialty* is a legitimate gift from God, and then uses it as he wants (without losing it), he can easily come to believe that he has already reached spiritual maturity (demonstrated by the manifestation of his gift—4:8). If so, his standing with God is validated for him by a special manifestation. Then he doesn't need to be concerned about immorality. He can easily adopt a false sense of security as did the Israelites who encountered the miraculous (10:1-13). They became careless because God was still in their midst, as seen by His manifestations. This "mature" person may think that he already knows all that is necessary (8:1). One with this attitude can easily become loose with his associations (10:14-22; II Cor. 6:14—7:1) and careless in worship (chapter 11). One can become so subjectively certain that he doesn't really *need* the objective verification of Jesus' resurrection (chapter 15). One's surety with God, validated by sensational spiritual gifts, can cause his relationship with his fellow Christians to take a back seat (It's God and me—that's all that counts).

Perhaps these attitudes (particularly the last one) are part of the *results* of misunderstanding and misusing spiritual gifts in the Corinthian church. It seems significant that Paul begins his discussion about spiritual gifts (chapter 12) immediately after dealing with the factions demonstrated at the Lord's Table (11:17-34, especially 12-22). Isn't it interesting that these people could be so rich in "gifts" and then live the way they did? Now let's look at the context leading up to chapter 14.

CHAPTER 12

Paul begins chapter 12 with a reminder that in their former paganism, the people had been led astray to what was not true (dumb idols) by various means (however you were led). The means of the leading included the use of wine, sex, spirit-possession, emotionalism seen in visions, ecstatic utterances, dreams, etc. (see E. R. Dodds, *The Greeks and the Irrational*). To be swept away by an apparent supernatural pull does not necessarily indicate a Christian source. This is a common phenomenon in pagan religions today. However, Paul does affirm that the gifts spoken of in chapters 12-14 are from God.

Paul then suggests that the legitimate gift from God is based upon knowledge, not sensationalism. The knowledge is seen in the confession that the historical Jesus *is* Lord (12:3). This confession cannot be made knowledgeable without encountering evidence. Responsible faith comes through the preaching about Jesus (Rom. 10:13-17; II Peter 1:3-11). Paul writes the confession of 12:3 in the vernacular language of his readers. One could not use this test if the confessor is using ecstatic or untranslated foreign languages. Thus at the outset, Paul bases the Christian's position not upon subjective experiences which can carry one away to unreality (12:2), but rather upon the intelligent acknowledgement of Jesus (See also I Peter 1:3).

Paul then develops the truth that God's gifts *(charismata)* vary (4-11). God gives to each Christian at least one *charisma* for the good of others (7). Our *charismata* are given for a ministry to others (service and workings, verses 5 and 6), not for ego-inflation. Each Christian should accept with thanksgiving what God has given to him, because his personal *charisma* is a result of the will of the Spirit (11). Thus our gifts are not due to our dedication, but rather to God's decision (12:11, 18, 24; Eph. 4:8; I Peter 4:10,11).

In verses 12 and 13, Paul begins to develop the analogy of the church being like a physical body—united amid diversity. Although she has many members, the body is still one. The many are one because each has been baptized into one body (Gal. 3:26-28; Eph. 2:11-22; 4:1-16). This unity has come by the influence of the Holy Spirit (John 16:8), and in that unity the Holy Spirit indwells (13). It is the Spirit within Christians which causes them to become *one body* (Eph. 4:3; Rom. 8:9, 14-17; Acts 2:38, 41; I Cor. 12:12,13).

In verses 14-31, Paul develops the unified way the various members of the Christian body should function for the mutual good (see the chapter on *The Christian's Charisma).* In 14-31, the following points are developed:

1. Every member is significant. This should check inferiority complex and envy (14-16).

2. It is not logical to demand conformity. As our body functions well because members *are different,* not because they are alike, so it is with the body of Christ. Conformity would actually destroy the body (17-20).

3. No one is functionally superior to another. This should help check a superiority complex. It is wrong to honor just the spectacular (21).

4. There is to be a unity of care. Special attention is to be given to the less sensational (22-25).

5. God has so arranged the organs (members) so they will not compete against one another, but complement one another (25 and 26).

6. No one is to covet another's gift, because

    a. God gave it,
    b. none has all gifts, and
    c. all should seek the best gifts (27-31).
In context, the *best gifts* surely refer to those which will best edify fellow members and *build up Christ's body* (12:7; 14:3, 4, 5, 6, 12, 19, 26, 31).

    The gist of 12:14-31 is that it is wrong to use our gift(s) in an individualistic way. It is *for others* that God has given each gift. This corresponds with God's own nature. He is love. It also corresponds with His first encounter with people. In the Garden, He shared with them His equipment so they could function. The kind of responsibilities God fulfills throughout the universe, He shares to a degree with man. God creates. He shared with man a purposeful, multiplying function. God sustains. He shared with man a caring function ("take care of the ground"). God dominates, and so He shared a bit of that function with man ("gave us a ministry of reconciliation"). *God's gifts to us are not to be used selfishly.* After Paul suggests that gifts are to be used unselfishly, he introduces chapter 13, the love chapter.

CHAPTER 13

    Agape-love is a love which (1) sees a need in another and moves to meet it, (2) doesn't count the cost, (3) doesn't calculate the return, (4) doesn't evaluate the worth of the one needing to be loved, and (5) always lives for the good of the other (this is demonstrated in Jesus' whole life as summed up in Romans 15:1-3; Phil. 2:1-11).

    In chapter 13, Paul develops the manner in which gifts are to be used, and thus develops more fully the truth of chapter 12. Spiritual gifts are to be used with *agape*-love, i.e., used for others. To fail to see this, results in an emphasis upon the gift and not upon the giver and His intention. It should be noted that love itself is a result of the Holy Spirit (Gal. 5:22; Rom. 5:5).

Paul then develops some characteristics of love (4-7) and the temporary nature of some gifts compared with the permanent nature of love (8-13, and see the chapter on *The Perfect of I Corinthians 13*).

If one will accept the truth of chapter 13, he should then accept the unselfish functional nature of the gifts in chapter 12, which is re-emphasized in chapter 14 in the consideration of tongues and prophecy. But if chapter 13 is not understood in its context, the teaching of diversity in chapter 12 will give way to the demand for conformity (and the idea of differing "levels" of Christians) and the restricted use of tongues in chapter 14 will be rejected. Only the *un*-selfish is willing to restrict self for the good of others. To emphasize the gifts which are temporary and neglect the way which is permanent (13:8, 13) is to major in minors and to minor in majors.

The characteristics of *agape*-love listed in verses 4-7 directly relate to the problem of misunderstanding and misusing spiritual gifts. These characteristics—being patient, being kind, being not jealous, not bragging, not being arrogant, not acting unbecomingly, not seeking its own, not being easily provoked, not taking into account a wrong suffered, not rejoicing in unrighteousness, but rejoicing in the truth—can be easily related to 12:14-31 and to chapter 14. To not do so is to miss their contextual significance. To illustrate: "Doesn't seek its own way" relates to 14:3; 12:21ff; "Patient" relates to 14:27, 28, 35; "Does not brag" relates to 12:11, 19 and 14:6 which further relates to 4:7.

CHAPTER 14

The transition from chapter 13 to 14 is so smooth that one hardly notices a chapter division. Since gifts are to be used for others (chapters 12 and 13), Paul develops in chapter 14 the value of prophecy over tongues (in helping others). To seek spiritual gifts is good, he says, but the aim in the seeking must be love for others (14:1, see also I Tim. 1:5). A good commentary for verse 1 is verse 12, "So also since you are zealous of spiritual gifts, seek to abound for the edification of the church." That admonition also fits chapters 12 and 13, which must be kept in focus as chapter 14 is read.

In verses 1-5, Paul develops the superiority of prophecy over other spiritual gifts. By use of the word *prophecy,* Paul seems to be referring to inspired preaching in a vernacular language for the purpose of revealing Christ (1:18—2:16).

The reason Paul emphasizes prophecy (v. 1) is because it builds up, holds up, and cheers up others (v. 3). It edifies insiders (5, 19) and evangelizes the outsiders (24, 25). However, untranslated languages confuse the outsiders and show the actual disbelief of insiders who demand that gift (21-23).

Verse 2 begins with "for" *(gar),* which introduces an explanation for saying "especially that you prophesy" (v. 1). The reason prophecy is of more value than languages is because no one understands untranslated languages but God. A good commentary on verse 2 is verses 10 and 11.

There is some uncertainty about the meaning of "in his spirit" in verse 2 (NASB). The word *his* is not in the Greek. A literal translation of the phrase is "he is saying a mystery in a spirit." The translation *"the* spirit" in RSV and KJV is not technically correct. It should also be noted that the

Greek case of *spirit* could allow the translation "*by* a spirit" or "*with* a spirit." The Greek word *pneuma* (spirit) is used in many ways in the Bible. In this verse, it probably refers to the sub-conscious faculty in man, i.e., that activity done without the cooperation of the speaker's understanding. (However, just what *spirit* means in verse 2 is problematic.) Verses 14 and 15 give some support for the spirit in this verse referring to a sub-conscious activity which bypasses man's understanding.

There is another interesting possibility for understanding the connotation of *spirit* in this verse. The word *pneuma* is a technical Greek term which can denote the musical sound produced by the blowing of human breath into an instrument. Paul may be suggesting that mysteries are being produced by man's sound—his vocal cords, but not by his mind (that is, vocal sounds used without real meaning). Schweitzer thinks this connotation has relevance, in this context, in the light of verses 7-9 which speak about musical sounds (See Schweitzer's article on *pneuma* in the *Theological Dictionary of the New Testament*.)

Some think verse 2 is speaking about a prayer language; however, Paul does not say that specifically. In verse 15, Paul refuses to engage in a prayer that uses an untranslated language. In verse 2 Paul seems to be referring merely to language/speech which is not understood by man (Just try yelling Fire! to a crowd in a foreign language and measure the results). In light of the fact that *glossa* (see chapter on *An In-Depth Look at the Word "Tongue" in the Bible*) refers to a known foreign language only, God would understand it even if men didn't.

While verse 2 shows the inferiority of untranslated

languages to prophesying (preaching), verse 3 shows the superiority of prophecies. Then verse 4 puts the reason for the contrast of values into one sentence. "One who speaks in a tongue edifies himself, but one who prophesies edifies the church." In light of chapters 12 and 13, I cannot agree that edifying *self only* is a desired activitiy IN THIS CONTEXT. Rather it is a use of the gift selfishly and thus violating the principles outlined in the two preceding chapters. The use of untranslated languages is self-serving while prophecy is self-giving. It cannot be denied that the manifestation of glossolalia (regardless of the form—ecstatic or languages) is therapeutic for many. To believe that any act is from God carries the real possibility of therapeutic value to the person. Edifying self may be and is for many a result of glossolalia but should not be the reason for using it in public. To do it at all *just to feel better* is a questionable scriptural purpose.

In verse 5 Paul says, "I now wish (better translated *I am willing*) that you all spoke in tongues." The statement must be understood in its context, which reveals: (1) tongues *(glossa)* was a gift from God in that day; (2) Paul has already implied in 12:27-30 that not all *will* or even *should* do it; (3) He will not forbid people speaking in tongues if they stay within the curbs he will soon outline—however, his preference is clear; (4) He urges them to seek the greater gifts (12:31) and stresses prophecy. Nowhere does he say, "seek tongues."

Verse 5 affirms that the one who is preaching in the vernacular language is greater than the speaker in an untranslated language. Only if the language is translated can it edify the church. Again the intention of God's gifts is seen—the equipment of others. The moment language is translated so it can be understood, it becomes prophecy. If the speaker himself translates one wonders about the need for the language for serving others. It is interesting that verse 5 talks about the speaker himself translating, and verse 13 urges him to pray to translate. Note that the word *someone* in the RSV text is not in the Greek, where the subject is the 3rd person singular pronoun, *he.*

In verses 6-12, Paul develops the explanation for the uselessness of untranslated languages—talk without understandable content does not benefit the hearer. When Paul says, "If I come to you speaking in tongues," he is not suggesting that he will do this (see verses 18 and 19). The Greek word for *if* suggests only a hypothetical possibility. But, nevertheless, if (unlikely) he would, he says that it would be of *no benefit* unless it had understandable content. The fact that it comes from the mouth of an apostle will not change that. This reinforces the latter point in verse 5, "our talk in the church is to edify others." Otherwise, it is like the random notes which come out of instruments. The meaningful distinctions of the tones and compositions are lost. A bugle is intended to communicate a message (e. g., taps, reveille, charge, retreat). But if the sound does not follow the patterns or compositions people know, it will not communicate (7, 8). The soldiers will think a child has gotten hold of the bugle (see verses 20, 23).

Paul makes his analogous conclusion in verses 10 and 11. Untranslated languages, like the bugle sound which no one has learned, do not communicate (9). Foreign languages are indeed just that—foreign! Thus, they do not serve. They may even aid in separation rather than uniting people, for the speaker becomes a barbarian to the hearer (10, 11). Paul then reminds the readers to be active in a building ministry (verse 12). This re-emphasizes chapters 12 and 13.

In verses 13-19, Paul transfers the idea of the uselessness of untranslated languages from a general setting (6-12) to a worship setting. Verse 13 is closely connected with verse 12 by the word *therefore,* which means "for this reason." Because languages not known by the hearers do not communicate (10, 11), and because the manifestations of the Spirit are for a ministry to others (12), a tongue-speaker must pray that he himself will translate. The verb *pray* is in the imperative mood—the mood of command. The literal translation is "therefore, the one who is speaking in a language must pray that he might translate." This introduces a tough restriction. It suggests that if the speaker doesn't know what he is saying, he is to keep silent—even if he is just praying!

In verse 14, Paul begins with the conditional sentence which suggests only hypothetically that he would do what he suggests (see comment on verse 6), "If (unlikely) I pray in a tongue (language) my spirit prays, but my mind is unfruitful." Immediately Paul then moves from the unlikely act to the likely act, "I shall pray with the spirit and I shall pray with the mind also." The category of speaking does not change the unfruitfulness to others if it is in untranslated languages. It might be talk *per se* (verse 2), praying (13), or singing (15). This is Paul's way to say that he will not engage in that which cannot be understood.

Should not *any act of worship* involve the total consciousness of the person? Isn't he to be aware what he is initiating? Is his understanding to be "left at home" while he worships? If so, how could he know he is confessing Jesus as

Lord (12:3)? In view of the fact that we shall be judged for every idle word, doesn't it behoove us to know the words we use? Does a yoga form of worship have a place in Christian worship if our God is a known person? Hasn't He made Himself known to us in an understandable way? He is real. To put our thoughts into meaningful words is to be responsible for them—shouldn't we? Then to offer them to God is indeed a meaningful act of praise coming from the depths of the whole person.

In verses 16 and 17, Paul shows that praying and singing in an untranslated language violates chapters 12 and 13. They do not meet another's need. "The other man is not edified" (17).

In verses 18 and 19, Paul gives us an insight to his conduct. He is not spotlighting the uselessness of untranslated languages out of a jealousy because he himself doesn't have the tongue-gift. He has it (verse 18), but will evidently never use an untranslated language—regardless of its source—in a public meeting. (Isn't a meeting public whenever another person is present whom we could edify?). We have no record that Paul ever used anything but the vernacular language (and we know of him preaching, praying, and singing). We would not know that he even had this tongue-gift were it not for this statement in verse 18. Christianity would probably fare better if others followed Paul's practice, for it follows the principles of chapters 12 and 13.

Paul would rather speak five understandable words in the hearing of others than ten thousand non-understandable words (19). But someone might ask, "If God understands, isn't that enough?" (2). But that misses the point. The point of these chapters is that God has called us to be ministers to one another.

In verses 20 through 25, Paul develops the significance (sign) of uninterpreted languages on the one hand and understandable prophecies on the other to the individual who hears either. Paul uses the present tense and the imperative mood at the outset of verse 20, which is best translated, *"Quit being children. . . ."* Could this suggest that to speak in non-understandable languages is like a small child who may say things he does not understand? Although verse 20 can relate to 14-19 in this way, it is more closely connected with verse 21.

Verse 21 is a very significant verse. The reference is to Isaiah 28:11. Isaiah speaks about God's people not being mature enough to listen to the objective word of God being spoken through His inspired prophets. The preached word was not enough evidence to convince them that God's promises were sure. Jews were known to demand signs for belief (I Cor. 1:22). In that attitude, they were like children who needed more than the parents' "words" to convince them (relate to verse 20). During the Isaiah 28 incident, many people turned their ears from meaningful content—the word of inspired prophets (28:12) to meaningless content—the words of false priests who were proud and drunkards (Isaiah 28:1, 7:10; see also Jeremiah 5, especially verses 15-31). God promised through the words of the prophets that the Assyrians would take over Israel if the people didn't repent; however, the verbal promises (and thus the ways of God) were not heeded.

Then the Assyrians did come! Their occupation and the presence of their *glossa* (language) served as an objective proof that the inspired prophets had been correct. But this event also revealed the disbelief of those who had needed more than the word. The Assyrian language to which I Cor.

14:21 and Isaiah 28:11 refer was a judgmental sign to the people of God who didn't believe God's word. "They would not hear" (Isa. 28:12). It was the failure to be open to God's preached word that brought this occupied foreign language which did not aid their belief. When we need more than God's word to believe his promises and power, faith is giving way to subjectivity. Then any word can get a hearing alongside God's word, depending upon which makes us "feel" better. This is precisely what happened in the incident to which 14:21 refers. Jeremiah 5:30, 31 puts it this way, "An appalling and horrible thing has happened in the land. The prophets prophesy falsely, and the priests rule at their own authority. And my people love it so! But what will you do at the end of it?" (NASB).

Any time we need more than the preached Word about the crucified Christ to convince us of God's love, we become open to the possibility of being led astray by the sensational, emotional, the intellectual, etc. (See I Cor. 12:1; and 1:18—2:5. In 2:4, the demonstration of the Spirit and power is the preached Word about Jesus. See 2:6-13. This preached Word is powerful—Rom. 1:16; 10:13,14; Eph. 6:18, John 16:8, John 12:48.)

From the Isaiah incident, Paul makes an analogy to the Corinthian situation in which people are evidently elevating the presence of foreign languages *above* the preached word. (Otherwise, there would have been no need to refer to Isaiah 28.) Paul concludes from the Isaiah 28 incident that "tongues are for a sign, not to those who believe, but to the unbelievers; but prophecy is a sign not to the unbelievers, but to those who believe" (v. 22, NASB). What does he mean by "unbelievers" and "believers" in verse 22? That he has a different people in mind than in 23 and 24 is obvious. In verse 22, Paul is not equating unbelievers with "outsiders" and believers with "insiders." As seen in the Isaiah 28 incident, both the believers and unbelievers are *inside* the pale of God's people. But there are two kinds of people inside—those who believe God's word is enough, and those who do not—these are the unbelievers in verse 22. They want something more. To seek something more is a confession that God's word *per se* is inadequate. To them, the resurrection of Jesus (chapter 15) is not enough evidence to say *"Jesus is Lord"* (12:3). Some find it hard to believe that the Word is powerful enough to convict people. Isaiah 28 makes it clear that when God brought in the foreign language, He recognized that this kind of people were not believing His words. They were immature (Isaiah 28:9). The Corinthians are also called immature (3:1; 13:11; 14:20). Prophecy, however, is a sign to the "believer." This is the insider who believes God's word *is* enough. God's verbal promises are validated because of the God who made them. To know that is enough.

In verse 23, Paul discusses the effect tongues have upon the unbeliever who is *not* within the membership of God's family. He makes it clear that he has switched to the outsider-kind-of-unbeliever by adding the word "outsider" (the word "outsider" is the Greek word *idiotes* which can also mean an unskilled person. Some take this meaning to refer to those fellow Christians who are unskilled in speaking in tongues because they do not have the gift. Thus these would not understand, but would rather consider their Christian brothers who spoke in tongues to be mad. This seems unlikely since Christians after Pentecost *did* affirm that this gift was from God.) It is the unbelieving *outsider* who would be turned off from God's power of salvation upon hearing untranslated languages in the assembly. He would think the group had gone mad (23). That is exactly what many thought about those in 1st century pagan religions who practiced ecstatic utterance.

However, if an outsider enters the assembly and hears preaching being done in his own language, he has contacted that form of communication which can convict him of his sins, permit him to acknowledge that God is present in the assembly, and then worship Him (24, 25). Thus, if we want people to see a demonstration of God's presence in our assembly the sure method is by the preaching of God's word in love. God honors His word. The Spirit works through His word. God's word is powerful. The following should be reviewed carefully: John 16:8, Eph. 6:17; Heb. 4:12; II Tim. 3:15,16; Titus 3:5; Rom. 1:16; 10:13-17; I Cor. 2:1ff; II Peter 1:3-11; Isa. 40:8; Psalm 119:19; Matt. 4:4; 8:16; John 8:31, 52; 14:23; 17:17; Acts 4:4; 8:4; Eph. 5:26; Phil. 2:16; Col. 3:16; II Tim. 4:2; I Peter 1:25.

In verses 26-33, Paul develops some orderly regulations for worship. He says that everything is to be done for edification. In context, that means by understandable language and in an orderly fashion (4, 11, 12, 13-19, 40). Orderly procedures as well as understandable language will aid the edifying process.

The procedures for the use of the gift of language are (1) no more than three people may use it during any public assembly (2) each user must speak in turn; (3) there must be a translator. If there is no translator, the gifted one is to keep silent. Could this suggest that he is to know about the presence of a translator in advance? Does one violate Scripture when he speaks publicly with only hopes that a translator is present?

Preaching also has orderly procedures to follow (29-33) as well as women (34-36).

Paul begins to conclude chapter 14 by putting responsibility upon those who think they are spiritual. If they are really spiritual, then chapter 14 should not be a problem for they will recognize this teaching as the Lord's command (37). But if one does not recognize this, then he himself is not recognized as being spiritual, regardless of the manifestations he displays (verse 28, and see also Matt. 7:21-24).

Paul concludes by urging the people to preach. However, he says, this does not mean that they are to forbid people using the gift of languages (39). But in context, the admonition *do not forbid* has restrictions attached to it. Paul has already outlined when the gift should not be used in public (28). Only if the qualifications of this chapter are met was the practice to be permitted in that day.

But how about today? Should the practice be allowed in public worship because of Paul's admonition in 14:39? This is a problematic position. In light of 13:8-13, the act today cannot be definitively supported as coming from God. The question is not if God *can* provide the gift. Of course He still has the power that provided it in the first century. But the question is, *"Does* He still?" To suggest that He does on the basis of Hebrews 13:8 ("Jesus Christ is the same yesterday, today, and forever,"), which is the major text for the longevity of tongues used by some Pentecostal Christians, is untenable. To take that position is to say that God could not begin something new nor end something. That position violates the God of history we read about in the Old and New Testaments. His ways *do* change. For instance, it isn't recorded that in the Old Testament or during the lifetime of Jesus, He gave anyone the gift of tongues. To let Heb. 13:8 be our dogma about tongues would mean that what happened in Acts 2 could not have happened because it had never happened before. We dare not fossilize God into that kind of thinking.

We do not deny that people are having experiences, nor that the experiences are helpful for some. Nor can we say, "It's from the devil" or "It's from God" (See chapters 6-8 in Burdick's *Tongues: To Speak or Not to Speak* for some good insights into possible explanations). However, those who do not believe that the phenomenon is still given by God should be very cautious about permitting it to be demonstrated in public worship. What one does in his own private devotion is another matter. No Christian has the right to force another's private devotion to fit his. Paul's admonition in verse 39, in context, refers only to speaking out in a public worship assembly. He has no word about a Christian's private practice. Our response to another who practices tongues in private is a matter of opinion. Let us not split Christ's body over opinions!

However, I would caution about the practice for these reasons—

(1) The need for the sensational to validate the love of God for you opens the door to dependency upon more and more sensationalism. It can become easy to stand upon personal sensational experiences rather than upon God's spiritual epistles. One can easily begin, without it being his plan, to evaluate the Bible by his experiences rather than to evaluate

his experiences by the Bible. It then becomes easy to believe that God will give visions, prophecies, and new revelations. The logical end to this is that if God does that today, we do not need His Word of 2000 years ago. That is the route some have gone. Perhaps it would be helpful to remember that ecstatic utterances, predictions about the future, the casting out of demons, healings, etc. are now being practiced commonly all over the world in pagan animistic religions, and those kinds of phenomena are not new. We have them recorded as early as 1400 years B.C. Jesus warned us not to depend upon the ability to do these special things for an evidence of being accepted by God (Matt. 7:21-23). He wouldn't even trust Himself to those who had to have signs for their trust (John 2:23, 24).

(2) The moment one lets his private practice be known, he is moving it into the public eye. The attitudes and defenses he uses to keep his practices may violate the principles outlined in chapters 12 through 14 of I Corinthians. May that *not* happen, for the good of Christ and His body (the church), for whom, because He loved us so much, He gave His life (Eph. 5:25). May we follow that example.

(3) "Signs and wonders" were given to apostles and prophets to authenticate them as Christ's messengers. These were "foundational" gifts. We need not keep on laying the foundation (see Acts 2:22; 4:30; 14:3; Romans 15:15-19; II Cor. 12:12; Hebrews 2:2-4).

The greatest sign of all is the resurrection. Each time Jesus was asked for a sign, he referred to the resurrection. Let us not lose sight of that as God's trans-cultural and trans-temporal evidence of His acceptance of us, and of His power in the world.

DISCUSSION QUESTIONS

1. Discuss the situation in the Corinthian church and relate the use of spiritual gifts to the situation.
2. What is the major point Paul is developing in I Corinthians 12:14-26?
3. How does the love chapter, I Cor. 13, relate to chapters 12 and 14?
4. What is Paul's main point in I Cor. 14?
5. Why is prophecy more significant than tongue-speaking?
6. What is the nature of tongue-speaking in I Cor. 14? Support your answer.
7. Why is an untranslated language useless?
8. What is the significance of Paul's reference to Isaiah 28?
9. Does I Cor. 14 gives us advice about tongue-speaking in privacy?
10. What does Paul say in I Cor. 14 about the significance of worship services? Relate this to what, why and how we should do activities in worship, whether or not they relate to tongue-speaking.

7

A LOOK AT SOME OF THE TEXTS AND LOGIC OF THE GLOSSOLALISTS

My original intention for this section was to write a comprehensive essay on the texts and logic used by glossolalists to support their position; however, it became apparent that this would require volumes to complete because the position of the glossolalists is not consistent. Therefore, I have limited this lesson to a consideration of some of the major positions held.

At a recent Society of Biblical Literature meeting, I asked a glossolalist scholar, "Who is the most objective pro-tongues writer today?" He promptly replied, "Larry Christenson." The *Renewal Magazine* called Christenson's book, *Speaking in Tongues,* "the best and sanest treatment of the subject we have seen." Perhaps the most renowned scholar among the glossolalists is David J. DuPlessis, who said that he would recommend Christenson's book with the greatest confidence wherever he goes. Therefore, I have decided to use Christenson's work as a primary source for this essay.

The amount of literature which is being published by the Pentecostals is surprising in light of the claim by many of them that the Holy Spirit is not a theology to be discussed and analyzed, but rather an experience to enter. Christenson takes that position (page 40), but yet writes 141 pages discussing and analyzing what he says should not be discussed and analyzed. He even gives advice for helping one to enter the experience. Some Pentecostals even claim that one proof that a man has received the baptism of the Holy Spirit is that he does not use notes in his preaching (Matt. 10:19 is cited). This usage of Matthew 10:19 is taken out of context. Jesus spoke it to his disciples on a particular occasion. The situation to which He refers is not preaching *per se,* but rather defense before a court. Jesus had told these particular disciples what they should preach (Matt. 10:7). They had been at His feet and were to proclaim what He had proclaimed. He Himself proclaimed what He had heard from His Father (John 5). The Christian is commanded to be diligent in his use of the Word (II Tim. 2:15). Application of Matt. 10:19 is not a "proof" that one is a Christian. If it is, then the Pentecostals who write about it betray their own position when they write books with footnotes quoting from other writers. The consistency of this position would require the opening of the canon. It is true that Jesus said to His apostles that the Holy Spirit would cause *them* to remember all that *He had said to them* (John 14:26); however, He did not say that to us. How could we remember something we did not hear? While the Holy Spirit completely furnished the apostles with the information they *had* encountered, the Bible furnishes us with information which we *have not* encountered (II Tim. 3:16,17).

Baptism of the Holy Spirit

The Pentecostals' central verse is Acts 2:4—"And they were all filled with the Holy Spirit and began to speak with other tongues, as the Spirit was giving them utterance" (NASB). Their central verse is Acts 2:4—"And they were all filled with the Holy Spirit and began to speak with other tongues, as the Spirit was giving them utterance" (NASB). Their central thesis is the baptism of the Holy Spirit with a special stress being placed upon the word "all" in Acts 2:4. To suggest that the word *all* refers to the one hundred twenty in 1:15 and is then to be applied to all subsequent Christians is highly problematic. In light of 2:7 and 14, the all seems to refer to the twelve apostles. It is the twelve that Peter is defending in 14ff. This cannot be determined by the Greek grammar—the argument that the nearest antecedent to the pronoun is the eleven apostles in 1:26 is not a valid argument from the standpoint of Greek grammar. But regardless of one's position on this, we cannot by Acts 2:1-4 alone suggest that all Christians in all generations are to receive the baptism of the Holy Spirit. This would be similar to saying that all will be fed fish and bread because all were in John 6. Further evidence must be considered. In this connection, it is interesting to note that those immersed on the day of Pentecost gave a different evidence of it than tongues (Acts 2:42-47).

SPIRITUAL GIFTS FOR CHRISTIANS TODAY

While Acts 2:4 is the central verse used by some to support the teaching of baptism of the Holy Spirit for all Christians, the entire book of Acts is used by them as supporting material. Christenson thinks that the central issue in Acts is the baptism of the Holy Spirit (page 57). That is certainly a problematic concept of the book of Acts and the manifestations of the Holy Spirit recorded there. Frank Stagg seems to be closer to the issue in Acts when he says that Acts is recording the unfettering of Christianity from Judaism. Luke is showing how Christianity is crossing many barriers to be the universal religion (*Acts of the Apostles*). The Holy Spirit is mentioned in Acts only once after 21:11. There are 11 (out of the 28) chapters in Acts where the Holy Spirit is not mentioned at all. The baptism of the Holy Spirit is directly referred to only twice. Thus it seems to be an over-reaction to say that this is *the central issue* in the entire book.

Some Pentecostals teach that a person's unity with Christ depends upon three different links:

1) repentance and faith,
2) water baptism, and
3) baptism with the Holy Spirit.

Christenson sees these three links in Acts 2:38 with "you shall receive the gift of the Holy Spirit" referring to the baptism with the Holy Spirit (page 48). Although Christenson believes that a person receives the Holy Spirit when he becomes a Christian, he thinks there is a fuller manifestation of the Spirit to come—the baptism with the Holy Spirit (a second grace). This is seen as a separate event from water baptism. The problem with this view is that both the New Testament and early church fathers speak of the reception of the

Holy Spirit as occurring at a water baptism which is an expression of faith in Jesus.

In his book *Baptism in the Holy Spirit,* Dunn rightly points out that the Pentecostals are correct in trying to teach that the Holy Spirit is to be experienced. Too many Protestant Christians lock up the Holy Spirit in a sacrament or in a book. We fail to teach that *the Holy Spirit dwells in us!* But Dunn also rightly points out that the Pentecostal attempt to restore the New Testament emphasis at this point has two unfortunate aspects—(1) A separation of the Spirit from conversion. It is contrary to New Testament teaching that the Holy Spirit is subsequent to Christian conversion. (2) A separation of faith from water baptism. About the Pentecostal, Dunn says,

> Conversion is for him Spirit-engendered faith reaching out to receive or accept Jesus, so that a man is a Christian before his water baptism and the latter is little more than a confession of a past commitment. This may well accord with present Baptist practice, but it is not the New Testament pattern. . . . *Baptism properly performed is in the New Testament essentially the act of faith and repentance—the actualization of saving faith without which, usually, commitment to Jesus as Lord does not come to its necessary expression.*

Dunn further says that baptism in the New Testament is the expression of faith to which God gives the Spirit (pages 226, 227). He expresses the New Testament teaching this way—

Faith demands baptism as its expression;
Baptism demands faith for its validity.
The gift of God's Spirit presupposes faith as its condition;

Faith is shown to be genuine only by the gift of the Spirit (page 228).

The Pentecostal position of second grace cannot be supported by New Testament teaching. In fact, Pentecostals are not consistent in identifying the time a person receives the "baptism of the Holy Spirit." Speaking in tongues is seen as the objective evidence which pinpoints the matter.

Christenson says that Scripture gives no consistent suggestion of any other objective evidence that a person has been *baptized* with the Holy Spirit (page 54). This is correct; however, Acts directly refers only twice to the *baptism* of the Holy Spirit about which John the Baptist spoke. It is at this point that Pentecostals err. They claim that the baptism of the Holy Spirit is seen five times in the book of Acts (chapters 2, 8, 9, 10, 19). Christenson takes this position; however, his position that only speaking in tongues is suggested by Scripture as evidence of the baptism of the Holy Spirit is weakened, because speaking in tongues is manifested in only three of these five (chapters 2, 10, 19). We must look a bit closer at the baptism of the Holy Spirit in the book of Acts.

All agree that Acts 2 fulfills John the Baptist's prophecy in Matthew 3:11. Jesus Himself makes the connection (Acts 1:4, 5). The only other event recorded in Acts which directly parallels the event in Acts 2 is found in Acts 10:44ff. This event is also directly connected with John's prophecy by Peter in Acts 11:15,16.

Just what was the significance of these events? Peter connects the baptism with the Holy Spirit (John's prophecy in Matt. 3:11) with the prophecy in Joel 2:28 (Acts 2:16ff). Joel is speaking about a new age to dawn which is to be signified

A LOOK AT SOME OF THE TEXTS AND LOGIC

by God pouring His Spirit upon all flesh. This will be the signal that the last days have *begun* (Acts 2:17). This beginning *begins* only once. From the standpoint of the Jews, "all flesh" referred to Jews and Gentiles. (To claim it means every individual fails to understand the usage of that day). However, the Spirit fell on only Jews on the Day of Pentecost; therefore, Joel was being initially fulfilled on that day. When the Spirit fell on the Gentiles in Acts 10, the prophecy was completely fulfilled. Or to put it another way, the last days were initially beginning in Acts 2, but in Acts 10 the last days *had begun*. Never again is John the Baptist's prophecy referred to in the New Testament.

God's Kingdom is then objectively open to all, to whoever calls on the name of the Lord. The Jews needed the demonstration of God's acceptance of the Gentiles to help them break through their prejudices. Paul makes this point clear in Acts 11:16,17. Other Jews agreed (verse 18). Thus the new age of God has fully begun. The Gentiles are included.

This in itself affirms that the Messiah has already come. For this Messianic era, with the inclusion of the Gentiles, was prophesied in Isaiah 11:10; 42:1, 6; 49:6, 22; 54:3; 60:3; 66:18-23; etc. This is the era in which God's Israel shall really function as God's ambassadors. God's objective acceptance of the Gentiles points to this prophecy being fulfilled. This is the primary significance of the baptism of the Holy Spirit. And *this is the significance of John's prophecy in Matt. 3:11.* He may not have known the significance of it, but Peter did. Note carefully that John's prophecy is not connected to any other event in the New Testament outside of the events in Acts 2 and 10. To connect it to any other event is a subjective application.

When Jews other than the twelve soon wanted to know how they could receive the Spirit, Acts 2:38 was spoken. When Gentiles other than Cornelius wanted to know, the early evangelists gave the same kind of response (see Acts, chapters 8 and 16). Since the Kingdom of God was now open to both Jews (Acts 2) and Gentiles (Acts 10), both enter into it via the same means. To see how God says this is done, read Acts 2:38; 3:12; 8:35-39; 9:17, 18; 11:24 (and see 2:41 for how people were "added"); 16:14,15, 30-33; 19:1-7; 22:16.

Every Christian received the Holy Spirit at his immersion, but not every Christian received a supernatural gift as a special manifestation. (But every Christian has received *charisma*—see Lesson 8). In some cases, supernatural manifestations came with the laying on of the apostles' hands (Acts 8, 19). We should not conclude that the Holy Spirit was not indwelling the Samaritans and John's disciples before hands were laid on them. If they were baptized in the name of Jesus, Acts 2:38 applies to them (and they had been—Acts 8:12; 19:5). They were given special gifts not by a *baptism* of the Holy Spirit, but rather by the laying on of the apostles' hands. In neither of these instances is there a reference to John's prophecy of Matt. 3:11. The same kind of thing did not happen in Acts 8 and 19 as happened in Acts 2 and 10.

In Acts, we see two different manifestations of the Holy Spirit received in three different ways. We must not cross categories. To lump everything into one designation is to miss the events the text records. Let's look at these two different manifestations of the Holy Spirit.

1) The *gift* of the Holy Spirit. This was received by faith,

repentance, and baptism (Acts 2:38). The purpose is for salvation (for a good study on this, read Seth Wilson's *Good News or Bad?* Mission Outreach). It is for anyone who calls on the name of the Lord (Acts 2:21; 22:16; Rom. 10:13). The result is seen in the fruit of the Spirit (Gal. 5:22ff), which energizes "ordinary" *charisma* in a Christian. Conversion enables ordinary charisma to be used unselfishly (II Cor. 5:15).

2) The *gifts* of the Holy Spirit (note a difference between gift and gifts). This was received in Acts in two different ways, which brought certain "special" gifts:

a) The baptism of the Holy Spirit prophesied by John the Baptist. This occurs in Acts 2 and Acts 10, and is so identified in Acts 1:4 and 11:15ff. This manifestation of the Spirit was to show that a new era in God's history had begun as prophesied in the O.T.

b) The laying on of apostles' hands. This was given to whom the apostles willed. It was given only to those who had already been immersed. Thus, the Holy Spirit was already theirs as an indwelling reality. This act bestowed special gifts which could be seen (Acts 8:14ff and 19:1ff).

There are differences in these special gifts. In (a) there was no laying on of hands, and the event was called the baptism to which John referred. In (b) there is a laying on of hands. That seems to be necessary. And the event was *not* called the baptism to which John referred.

It is interesting that the baptism of the Holy Spirit came when the two major groups were being accepted (Jews and Gentiles) and the laying on of hands was administered after two minority groups within Judaism were evangelized. We cannot say definitely that apostolic hands *had to be laid on* people before they received special charismatic gifts, but *that is the only way we know for certain* that special charismatic gifts came, after the initial baptism of the Holy Spirit to the Jews and Gentiles.

To call every instance of the Holy Spirit in Acts a baptism of the Holy Spirit is to mix categories and to call certain phenomena by a designation which the apostles did not. It is, further, to drain away the significance of the baptism of the Holy Spirit. Perhaps we should look at Paul's experience in Acts, since some say he experienced the baptism of the Holy Spirit.

The event in Acts 9 does not suggest a baptism with the Holy Spirit. It is not at all similar to the baptisms of the Holy Spirit described in Acts 2 and 10. God revealed to Paul that Ananias' hands were being laid on him for healing (9:12). But when Ananias came to Paul, he said, "Brother Saul, the Lord Jesus who appeared to you on the road by which you came, has sent me that you may regain your sight *and be filled with the Holy Spirit*" (9:17). So Paul was to receive two things. And Ananias did two things for Paul—he laid his hands on him, and he baptized him (verse 18). God wanted Paul to know that the laying on of hands was to restore his sight (verse 12 makes this clear by the use of a result clause). After Ananias laid his hands on Paul (verse 17), we are told that Paul received his sight (18a), but we are not told that he then received the Holy Spirit. Why? Because he had not. He received the Holy Spirit as a result of the next act, "Then he rose and was baptized" (18b). This fits the teaching of Acts 2:38 and 22:16.

Pentecostals claim that Paul had to receive the baptism of the Holy Spirit because of Acts 2:4 and Acts 2:39. The promise of Acts 2:39—"For the promise is for you and your children, and for all who are far off, as many as the Lord our God shall call to Himself," must be read in the context of Acts 2:38. It is *that promise* which is for all—not the promise recorded in Acts 1:4, 5. The Holy Spirit is promised to those who, out of faith, repent and are immersed. There is no hint for the need of a second kind of action such as asking for a fuller blessing. Acts 2:38 *does not say* "Repent, be immersed, and then ask and you shall receive the Holy Spirit" (suggesting that not all Christians receive the Holy Spirit, which is the Pentecostal position). But rather the text says, ". . . you *shall receive* the gift of the Holy Spirit." That is God's promise.

It is *acceptance of His promises* that brings us salvation (II Peter 1:4). That water baptism is connected with the reception of the Holy Spirit is suggested in such places as Acts 2:38; John 3:5; I Peter 3:21; Romans 6: Col. 2:12-3:1; I Cor. 12:12,13; Gal. 3:27 (and see 3:1). Some feel that Paul *had to receive the baptism* of the Holy Spirit to be an apostle; however, that was *not* a qualification of an apostle (Acts 1:21ff says what was required), and Paul never refers to such a baptism in defending his apostleship. How did Paul receive supernatural powers? We don't know. The text is silent. We note however that no mention is made of his working any miracles until after he was with the other apostles in Jerusalem. Did they lay their hands on him?

Different Baptisms

Some Pentecostals suggest that one main difference between water baptism and the baptism with the Holy Spirit is that *man is doing the baptizing in water, but Jesus is doing the baptizing* in the Holy Spirit baptism. John certainly did say that Jesus would baptize with the Holy Spirit. And He did. Peter says that it is Jesus who poured out the Spirit on the day of Pentecost (Acts 2:33). However, this does not mean that the gift of the Holy Spirit which God promised in water baptism does not *also come from Jesus!* The Holy Spirit *is* the Spirit of Christ (Rom. 8:9). If He came from Christ, Christ *must have given Him.* He is a gift, a gift from Jesus Christ.

The Spirit Within

The Pentecostals are correct to suggest that Acts 1:8 shows that Christian witnessing comes after the Holy Spirit is a part of man; however, that text does not say that the Holy Spirit comes to all in the same way He came to the twelve. Peter answered in Acts 2:38 how He is available to all. Perhaps we have not taught people well enough about the power which begins to live in them when they are born into Christ's Kingdom. We talk more about receiving forgiveness through faith, repentance and baptism than about the gift of the Holy Spirit which is then given. We speak so often about being babes in Christ that Christians act like babies too often, too long. Reluctance to witness can be a learned response. It is not the baptism of the Holy Spirit which is necessary for effective witnessing, but the *power of the Holy Spirit.* And that divine nature (and power) is ours as we accept and act upon God's promises (II Peter 1:4)!

Glossolalists generally agree that baptism of the Holy Spirit comes after (sometimes at the same time as) one becomes a Christian, by his asking specifically for that baptism. Luke 11:13 is their key text. *"If you then, who are evil, know how to give good gifts to your children, how much more will the heavenly Father give* the Holy Spirit *to those who ask him."* It is interesting that the parallel text (Matthew 7:7-11) does not say *Holy Spirit* but rather *good things.* One must be cautious about claiming too much (or too little) from Luke 11:13. This is *not an automatic answering service* from God. Jesus prayed that His disciples be kept from the evil one, but not all were. Paul wanted his thorn in the flesh to be taken away, but it wasn't. Simon asked for a special ability, but was refused (Acts 8:18ff). James said, "You ask and do not receive" (James 4:1). Our prayers must be in accordance with God's will. If my understanding of I Cor. 13:8 is correct, it is superfluous to pray for tongues.

How to Receive the Spirit

But the even bigger question is—*How does one ask for the Holy Spirit?* And note that Luke does *not* say to ask for baptism of the Holy Spirit. Didn't those on the Day of Pentecost ask for the Spirit when they called out, "What shall we do?"(Acts 2:37). Peter answered them with how to receive the Holy Spirit. Didn't the Ethiopian nobleman ask when he exclaimed, "Look! Water! What prevents me from being baptized?" (Acts 8:36). Didn't Paul ask when he inquired, "What shall I do, Lord?" (Acts 22:10). Didn't Cornelius ask when, after summoning Peter as God directed, he said, "Now then, we are all here present before God to hear all that you have been commanded by the Lord" (Acts 10:33)? Didn't Lydia ask when she "opened her heart to respond to the things spoken by Paul" (Acts 16:14)? Didn't the jailer ask when he said, "Sirs, what must I do to be saved?" (Acts 16:30). To ask for the Holy Spirit *is to ask for sanc-*

tification; it is to ask for justification; it is to ask for salvation; for no one is a Christian *without the Spirit of Christ* (Rom. 8:9).

Although Christenson depends heavily upon Luke 11:13, he seems to betray belief in it when he writes, "a person may be coached into speaking in tongues." Christenson even says that God is ready to give this gift, but we do not know how to receive it (page 128). That goes beyond Luke 11:13. Christenson then rationalizes going beyond simple asking to the dependence upon other means, by saying, "If the gift becomes knit into their prayer life in a wholesome way and brings forth the fruit of edification, then we cannot score too seriously the particular way in which they prayed for and received the gift" (128). In other words, the end justifies the means.

Christenson then spends four pages giving instructions on how to speak in tongues (129-132). He lists four steps, none of which were present in any of the Acts accounts, and all of which go beyond Luke 11:13. These four steps are:

1) Search Scripture;
2) Ask, "Why do I want it?"
3) Tell God you want it; and
4 Quit speaking in your native language.

Christenson says it is good to seek out someone who already has experienced "the blessing" and have him pray with you. I cannot find that anyone who spoke in tongues in Acts searched Scripture for it, asked for it, questioned the motive for wanting it (or even did want the gift), or began to speak expecting it. The only one who actually is spoken of as wanting the gift was rebuked for it (Acts 8:18ff). Christenson suggests that a person need not understand what he is doing. He also suggests that *Jesus didn't understand His baptism, but did it anyway* (page 38). I find that to be unacceptable in light of Matt. 3:15!

THE VALUE OF TONGUES

Pentecostals list the following values for speaking in tongues:

1. Speaking in tongues is the only sure objective evidence of the Holy Spirit (they say). Since tongues are recorded only three times in the book of Acts, and nowhere else outside the Corinthian church, I find this to be a problematic postition to take. Joy and witnessing seem to be a more universal evidence in Acts, than tongues. It is true that people should see the demonstration of the Spirit in our lives. We are to demonstrate the new life which comes from the Spirit (read Romans 6). Paul demonstrated it by his preaching (Acts 9:20). The Ethiopian eunuch showed it by his joy (Acts 8:39). Lydia showed it by her hospitality (Acts 16:15). The jailer showed it by his fellowship and joy (Acts 16:34). The first Christians showed it by their fellowship and sharing (Acts 2:42-47). The Thessalonian Christians showed it by their work of faith, labor of love, and endurance of hope (I Thess. 1:3). Timothy showed it by going with Paul to preach (Acts 16:1-3). The *new life* is the demonstration that we have received the Spirit (Rom. 6; Col. 2:12ff; Gal. 5:25ff).

2. Speaking in tongues gives a new dimension in worship. I Cor. 14:2,3 is used as the basis for this position. It is believed that tongue-speaking makes contact understandable with God. However, Paul said that *he wouldn't pray in tongues* in a public worship service (I Cor. 14:14, 15). To claim that this

act *makes contact understandable with God* comes close to making God totally transcendent! Jesus taught His disciples to pray in their vernacular language (Matt. 6:9ff).

Christenson says that one of the greatest blessings to the Christian is *when he has no idea what he is praying*. He says that the blessing is in knowing that the limitation of our mind is bypassed. He seems to suggest that the prayer which begins in the depths of a man's soul becomes perverted when it passes through "a maze of linguistic, theological, rational, emotional, and personal check-points" (page 73). It is true that we can tend to be dishonest in our praying, but the solution to that does not come through bypassing our thoughts, but rather through realizing that God already knows us and accepts us, and then being honest with Him. This is confession. Rather than being more honest with God, the use of tongues bypasses the very means which God gave us to be honest with Him. To cover up your language so that you do not even understand it *is surely not to face God* squarely with the self.

Christenson even suggests that *one can pray this way while having his mind on something else*. He suggests that one can "pray without ceasing" by praying in tongues, "since praying in this way leaves the mind free to concentrate on routine tasks" (page 74). I would be more inclined to call that a mixed devotion to Christ—a divided devotion against which Paul warns in II Cor. 11:3.

Praying in tongues is considered by many to be the prayer of God's Spirit. Rom. 8:26, 27 is used as a proof text; however, that text speaks about an intercession which the Spirit does on our behalf which is *not uttered*—"to deep for words."

A LOOK AT SOME OF THE TEXTS AND LOGIC

This bypass of the human mind is particularly difficult to accept when Christenson connects the way one expresses his tongue-speaking with the way the mind has been trained! He says,

> The manner in which a person expresses the gift of tongues is not determined primarily by the gift itself. It is largely determined by the individual himself, and by the religious setting. If a man worships in a religious setting where the emotions are expressed in a loud and exuberant fashion, and if he himself is similarly inclined, then he will likely express speaking in tongues in this way (page 82).

To bypass the mind is to *not take seriously* the admonition of Rom. 12:2, "be transformed by the renewing of your mind"; and Matt. 22:37, "love the Lord your God with . . . all your mind"; and I Peter 1:13, "gird your minds for actions." To speak one thing and be thinking another could easily develop into a situation close to that described in Matt. 15:8, *"This people honors Me with their lips, but their heart is far away from me."* Since we will be judged by every word spoken (Matt. 12:37 says we will be), it behooves us to *know what we are speaking*. The prayers of Jesus, the early church, and the Psalmist, were all uttered in a vernacular language.

3. Speaking in tongues takes away bad habits (page 78). We do not find this promise anywhere in the Bible. But rather we find such admonitions as Col. 2:1ff and 3:1—4:6; Gal. 5:25—6:10; Eph. 4:1—6:20; Phil. 2:1-13; Rom. 6; Romans chapters 12-14; etc. *All these indicate personal responsibility and need for attentive commitment.*

4. Speaking in tongues makes one certain about salvation (page 77). The Holy Spirit is certainly God's first installment of His salvation to us (Eph. 1:13, 14; II Cor. 1:21, 22). However, a need for "tongues" to give the assurance, as Christenson here claims, is problematic. How often in the New Testament is tongue-speaking suggested as a means to know whether a person is saved? We should study carefully I Peter 1:20-22; II Peter 1:3-13 and I John 5:11, 12! The entirety of I John is answering the question, *"How can I know I am a Christian?"* And he somehow fails to mention even one word about speaking in tongues!

5. Speaking in tongues is for self-edification (74ff.). Christenson says that the edification of the total person is in view (76). However, that contradicts the fact that he has previously said that the use of tongues bypasses the mind (74, 75). Is the total person edified by circumventing use of the mind God gave the person?

The Universality of the Gift of Tongues

Although Christenson affirms the existence of various gifts of the Holy Spirit, he places tongues as the one *all should have.* This violates I Corinthians 12, which speaks of the diversity of gifts. These other gifts are never suggested by Christenson as being for all Christians. We have no right to suggest that a particular one in the I Cor. 12 list is superior to others (except as an inspired writer makes determination). That practice may have been the cause of the problem in that church. Paul speaks directly against the practice. Christ apportions the gifts *as He wills,* not as we desire or dictate (I Cor. 12:11).

Trials of the Tongue-Speakers

Christenson suggests two universal trials that will come after one has begun to speak in tongues:

A LOOK AT SOME OF THE TEXTS AND LOGIC

1) The first trial is *doubt*. Christenson says that the first reaction is usually, "I am just making this up." He says this is a natural thought, for the inter-action between the believer and the Holy Spirit is so subtle that it is hard to draw a clear line between my speaking and His prompting. He suggests that the temptation when this thought comes is to draw back and deny the gift, or quit using it (131).

This is a hard explanation to square with the Acts accounts. There is no mention of any of those who spoke in tongues doubting what they were doing. It is even more difficult to square with Christenson's earlier statement that "it is never *assumed* that a person has been baptized with the Holy Spirit. When he has been baptized with the Holy Spirit, the person *knows* it" (page 38). Rather than doubt, Christenson has previously seen it as a tool for confidence and joy—the *assurance that he has received* the Spirit!

2) The second trial Christenson sees is *the fading of joy* which comes after the initial gift. "It doesn't seem to be doing anything for you" (page 131). Christenson says that God does that on purpose because He wants people to grow to the point where they act according to faith and not feeling (132). However, the Bible doesn't teach that we begin with God on feeling which allows us to grow so we can act on faith. Rather, God teaches that we begin on faith, and the result of the faith is joy—not vice versa! Fellowship in Christ's body is to bring complete joy, not fading joy (I John 1:4).

Pentecostals have been correct in calling all Christians to take seriously the work of God's Holy Spirit. However, to posit a second work of grace, the equation of the filling of the Holy Spirit with the baptism of the Holy Spirit, the demand for tongue-speaking as an objective evidence that one has the Holy Spirit—these are scripturally questionable positions. A new dimension in this problem is coming to light—Glossolalists are beginning to identify other glossolalists as brothers "in Christ" regardless of other doctrinal positions. This is crossing many barriers which had separated Christian men, but it is also erecting a new barrier to fellowship *in Christ*. May the body of Christ never use tongues as the means to identify another person as a Christian. One who has the Spirit of Christ belongs to Christ, and so is a brother to every other Christian.

DISCUSSION QUESTIONS

1. Can the concept of a "second grace" (in reference to a supposed "baptism of the Spirit" thought to occur later as Christian growth continues in the Christian) be Biblically supported? Why?

2. Discuss the baptism of the Holy Spirit. What is it? What is the significance of it? Where are records of its occurrence found in the Bible? Which accounts in Acts omit mention of this Holy Spirit baptism? Explain other gifts of the Spirit which are **not** this baptism.

3. When does a person receive the Holy Spirit? How do you know when you have received Him?

4. Can Christenson's four steps for initiating speaking in tongues be found practiced in the N.T.? What does this fact suggest about the value of the steps?

5. Is bypassing the mind in prayer really worshiping with the whole mind as Jesus commanded?

6. Name values, principles and/or practices which have rightly been called to our attention by some tongue-speakers. Which has been wrongly emphasized?

8

THE CHRISTIAN'S CHARISMA

No Christian wants to be left outside the pale of God's *charisma* (gift) and no Christian is. Every Christian has *charisma* (gift); however, he may not recognize a gift (or the absence of a gift) in others. This creates possible problems:

1) An inferiority complex sets in. If we see someone else with a *charisma* we lack, it is a natural tendency to feel cheated, to wonder, "Why am I left out? Perhaps I've not been receptive to *all* God has for me."

2) A desire for an objective manifestation sets in. Without recognizing any *charisma* in self, we can easily look for a "proof" that God has power for me.

3) A superiority complex sets in. If we see a *charisma* which we have, but find none in another, or one not as "potent" as ours, we can easily begin to think, "I'm a more full

Christian than that person. If he would accept what I have, he would become a more joyous Christian."

This methodology of comparing self with another person is condemned by Paul in II Cor. 10:12 "... *when they measure themselves by one another, and compare themselves with one another,* they are without understanding."

It is clear in I Cor. 12:4-11; I Peter 4:10,11; and Rom. 12:3-6 that God's *charismata* (gifts, plural form of *charisma)* to individuals differ. There is a variety. We are not to seek for conformity. The differences lie first of all in God's will for us, not in our inferiority or superiority (I Cor. 12:11; I Peter 4:10; Rom. 12:6; I Cor. 12:18, 27). It is a mark of mature faith to accept God's *charisma* with thanksgiving rather than with misgivings because the gift may not be what we expected, or what we see in others. To demand (anxiously, and then disappointedly) them ALL (or to select a certain gift or gifts as something I MUST HAVE) is anti-Scriptural. Paul makes it clear that not everyone has all God's *charismata* (I Cor. 12:29, 30). The healthy Christian is the one who joyfully accepts himself without being disappointed that he is not like another, and then functions with his God-given *charisma*. Whatever *charisma* God has given us is to be used, not abused, neglected or despised.

To be used how?

1) for another (I Peter 4:10);
2) for the common good (I Cor. 12:7);
3) for mutual care (I Cor. 12:26).

This fits the concept that Christian living is to be *agape* style (love) living. That kind of love (*agape*) seeks to meet the needs of others. This also fits the concept of Rom. 15:1-3, "We who are strong ought to bear with the failings of the

weak, and not to please ourselves; let each of us please his neighbor for his good, to edify him. For Christ did not please himself . . ." (RSV). This also fits the teachings of II Cor. 5:15 which says that the result of becoming a Christian is that we no longer live for self, but for Christ. In that context, living for Him involved:
1) evaluating people correctly, verse 16;
2) being righteous, verse 21; and
3) being a minister of God, verses 17-20.

God's *charisma* or *charismata* to any Christian is given precisely so we will *function as His ministers!*

Paul compares individual Christians in the church with individual organs in a physical body (Rom. 12:3ff.; I Cor. 12:12-26). Each organ in our body has its own function. Its *uniqueness makes* that organ important. The importance is seen in the function. The function of each organ is significant because it supplies a need to the other organs by doing what it alone can do. When any individual organ in the body, or Christian in the church, fails to function with its own *charisma,* it contributes to the deficiency of surrounding organs, or other Christians in the simile. If any organ decides to copy the *charisma* of some other organ, it becomes an organ not needed. If any organ decides it's going to call "cell meetings" in order to urge the other cells to be like it is, it then introduces "cancer" and ultimately destroys the body instead of contributing to its welfare. (Any cell in our physical body which does not function in accordance with its genetic code is unhealthy, and will eventually die and destroy surrounding cells if not checked.)

Christians in the church are the same way. The church is called "the body of Christ" and He is head of the body. As the body of Christ, the church must respond to the directing of the head. When each member does his part, this is a mutual harmony of joy and blessing in God's service. All the interests Jesus had and has, His body must, of course, have. However, no single individual has all His interests. Therefore, God calls different individuals with various interests, abilities, talents *(charismata)* to do His will. He puts us into His body partly because of a particular *charisma* (or *charismata*) which He wants to see function in and through His body.

It is the task of the church leaders to equip, help, and direct the members (individual cells) to function with the *charisma* God has given them. Only then can each member do the work of the ministry (Eph. 4:11,12). And it is only as each Christian functions in accordance with his God-given *charisma* that the body grows and remains in health. This is because God's means of supplying the needs of individual Christians is not by giving each one ALL His various kinds of *charismata,* but by giving to each Christian at least one. God then supplies *my needs* by giving to another Christian attributes which can meet my need. It is as *that Christian functions* that my need is met (Eph. 4:16; Col. 2:19). And as I function, I supply one or more of his needs. Like cells in our physical body, each one is equipped in ways that enable him to supply neighbor cells with nutrition as he functions (read I Cor. 12:12-16; Eph. 4:11-16; I Pet. 4:7-11).

This design from God gives to us one of the main reasons Christians are to congregate, fellowship, and share (Heb. 10:23-25). We belong to each other, and we *need each other.* Our responsibility is not only to win the world, but also to minister to the needs of those who are already Christians. In fact, we cannot do the first without the second. Christians cannot be involved in a ministry of reconciliation unless fellow Christians are supplying their various needs. Our love is to begin with the household of faith (Gal. 6:10). The unity we have in Christ is to be maintained (Eph. 4:3). Our care for one another is to be of prime importance to each of us (Rom. 12:9-21; Col. 3:12-17; Eph. 4:25-32; Gal. 5:25—6:6; I Thess. 5:14; Phil. 1:27, 28; 2:1-11). We are to *serve one another* through the *charisma* God has given to us. A *charisma* without the suffering servant kind of love *which gives self away for the brother* is useless (I Cor. 13:1-3).

The very *purpose* of each one receiving *charisma* is to serve others (I Cor. 12:12ff). To use the gift to edify self only is possible (I Cor. 14:4), but not advisable (I Cor.14:1-3, 5-19). To use any *charisma* for self-gratification is immature (I Cor. 12:20ff) because *the Christian is not to live for self* (II Cor. 5:15; Rom. 12:1-3; Phil. 2:1-11). But it is as we give ourselves in service to others that our own needs are met. In that action, we find meaning; in that activity, we mature; in that conduct, we find ourselves and enter the abundant life.

Now comes the big question—*What is God's charisma?* It is at this point that much misunderstanding has emerged, and has plunged many Christians into despair, frustration, anxiety and a sense of inferiority. This misunderstanding has caused many to become dissatisfied with themselves and want to be like someone else.

Some have a narrow concept of God's *charisma,* limiting it to a few manifestations of a supra-human kind. This concept can be paralyzing to the vibrant functioning of Christians.

Some of the arguments for tongue-speaking overlook the

usage of *charisma* in places outside of I Corinthians. In fact, Christenson (who is considered to be one of the most objective pro-tongue writers) says, "Is speaking in tongues the only valid objective manifestation that a person has had this definite instantaneous experience of the baptism with the Holy Spirit? Scripture does not say that it is the only one. But . . . scriptures give us no consistent suggestion of any other." For Christenson, tongue-speaking is the only valid sign that one has the Holy Spirit. He calls the current revival of tongue-speaking the "return of the charismata." Christenson here shows a lack of objective scholarship. To discover what God's *charisma* is, let us look at the word and its usage in the New Testament.

God's Charisma

The Greek word *charisma always indicates that which grace produces. Grace (charis)* is an action word (the *is* ending) and the corresponding result of that action is *charisma (ma* is a result ending in Greek). *Any person who has received God's grace has at the same time received God's charisma.* But something of what he has received may vary from what another has received.

The word *charisma* is used seventeen times in the New Testament. Although the grace is from God, it is problematic whether it refers (unless for its questioned use in I Corinthians) to a supra-human kind of manifestation. "Prophecy" in Rom 12:6 is probably an exception; however, that may refer to preaching without a direct inspiration being involved. Also see note below on usage in I Timothy. New Testament uses of *charisma* with identification of what each *charisma* is are here listed.

THE CHRISTIAN'S CHARISMA

Text	Identification of the Gift
Rom. 1:11......	encouragement (verse 12)
Rom. 5:15......	reconciliation—seen in justification, salvation, acquittal, righteousness, and eternal life (verses 6-18)
Rom. 6:23......	eternal life
Rom. 11:29....	mercy
Rom. 12:6-8...	prophecy, service, teaching, exhortations (or ability to comfort), monetary contributions, aid, acts of mercy
I Cor. 7:7.......	ability to remain unmarried (and need to marry)
I Cor. 12:5-10.	utterance of wisdom, utterance of knowledge, faith, healing, working of miracles, ability to distinguish between spirits, tongues, interpretation of tongues
I Cor. 12:31....	love (see I Cor. 13)
II Cor. 1:11....	answered prayer
I Tim. 4:14.....	ministry—note that if a special manifestation as in I Cor. 12:8-10 was given to Timothy, it is not indicated (we can't be dogmatic in identifying this gift to Timothy)
II Tim. 1:6.....	ministry
I Peter 4:10....	speaking, service (verse 11)

While some relate *charisma* only to gifts of the Spirit, it is interesting to note that another Greek word is always used when direct reference to the Spirit is made. That word is *dorea* (see Acts 2:38; 8:20; 10:45; Heb. 6:4). However, *dorea* is not a different quality of gift from *charisma*. The two words are used interchangeably. Evidence for this follows:

Although *charisma* is the result of *charis, dorea* is also called God's grace *(charis)*. See Eph. 3:7; 4:7; II Cor. 9:15. The interchangeableness of the two words is clearly seen in Romans 5:15, where both words are used in the same verse to refer to the same thing.

"But the free gift *(charisma)* is not like the trespass. For if many died through one man's trespass, much more have the grace of God and the free gift *(dorea)* in the grace of that one man Jesus Christ abounded for many" (RSV). The interchangeableness of these two terms is further seen in the fact that the same kind of gift is referred to by each—

charisma		*dorea*
Rom. 5:15	reconciliation	Eph. 4:7
I Tim. 4:14; II Tim. 1:6	a ministry	Eph. 3:7
Rom. 6:26	eternal life	John 4:10
Rom. 12:6	involvement of grace	II Cor. 9:15

What conclusions can we draw from this? (1) *Charisma* is not a gift with greater quality than any other kind of gift from God. (2) *Charisma* simply refers to whatever we receive from God. (3) The reference to a supra-human kind of gift is scarce. (4) God's gifts differ with individuals according to His will. (5) To seek for a gift He has not given, or to not use a gift He has given to us, is to question the wisdom, grace and will of God. (6) God's *charismata* may be categorized as—

A) Those universal gifts which all Christians in some degree possess: reconciliation, eternal life, the Holy Spirit, a ministry, love, joy, peace. All these are related. Eternal life is a quality of life for now as well as eternity. It results from reconciliation. With reconciliation, God gives a ministry (II

THE CHRISTIAN'S CHARISMA

Cor. 5:17ff). The Holy Spirit equips us to live the reconciled life with love, joy, and peace. (See Gal. 5:22, 23 for more universal gifts).

B) Those individualized gifts which are given to individuals by God to be used in and for His body! These individualized gifts are used through the ministry we perform. They vary because of the needs of people. They are related to the owner's personality, ability, talents, etc. They come under two categories:

1) Those which were foundational and thus temporary (I Cor. 12:8-10, and see the lesson on I Cor. 13:10).

2) Those which are functional and thus lasting. These are the various abilities which meet the kind of needs fellow members of the body have and will always have. These have not ceased with the coming of the completed revelation. In fact, the preaching of the revelation has the development of these in mind (I Tim. 1:5). These kinds of gifts are referred to in Rom. 12:4-9; Eph. 4:7-16, and I Peter 4:10,11. Each individual has at least one gift in this category to be used in his ministry to others. It may be the ability to teach, to give liberally, to comfort, to give benevolent aid, to do acts of mercy, to preach, to sing, etc. God has provided that what Jesus began, through the diversity in the membership, His body would continue to do and to teach (Acts 1:1; Eph. 1:23; 3:9, 10, 21).

The functioning of every Christian is important to God. Each Christian has been blessed by God through His grace. Our individualized differences are results of that grace (I Cor. 4:7; Eph. 4:7-9). We should thank God for our diversity and should endeavor to maintain our differences as well as our unity, for it is in our differences that the varying needs of the body are met (I Cor. 12:12-26).

Let us therefore keep a positive attitude about our individuality. Let us get on with manifesting the fruit of the Spirit (Gal. 5:22, 23) through our differences (Rom. 12:6-8). Let us accept not only God and His Son, but also the self which He has given to us. And may that self be committed to Him who is the head, and to His body (that is, to our fellow-members of the body) for the sake of winning the lost world which He came to save and to whom He sends us.

We do not need a supra-human manifestation to know that *God loves us* and has given us His Spirit, His *charisma,* and His ministry. The objective demonstration that He has is seen in His chief verification—the resurrection of Jesus and then our resurrection in Him (Romans 6). What we need is to know that the mind of the flesh must be subjected to and renewed by the mind of God's Spirit (Rom. 8:5-9, and see also 6:1-11 and 7:4). This agrees with I Cor. 12:13 which says that all are baptized into the one body and in that baptism are made to drink of the one Spirit (see Acts 2:38; Gal. 3:26, 27; Titus 3:5).

Every Christian has the *charisma* which is, and which results from, his new birth in Christ. Let us each live as one who expresses God's gift in the attitude of God's grace.

DISCUSSION QUESTIONS

1. What does **charisma** mean?
2. Who, in the biblical meaning, had **charisma**?
3. Do all Christians have the same **charisma**?
4. What are some **charismata**?
5. Why have some Christians doubted that they really do have **charisma** without some special manifestation?
6. Relate the use of **charisma** to church growth.